ANGELS
DEMONS
AND THE DEVIL

A CONVERSATION WITH MICHAEL THE ARCHANGEL ABOUT CELESTIAL BEINGS

F. LaGard Smith

cotswold publishing

ANGELS, DEMONS, AND THE DEVIL

Copyright © 2012 by F. LaGard Smith
Published by Cotswold Publishing
1509 Stratford Hall Circle
Murfreesboro, TN 37130

Distributed by 21st Century Christian
2809 Granny White Pike
Nashville, TN 37204

ISBN 978-0-9660060-6-3

Cover design by Jonathan Edelhuber

Anonymous, 15th century, Saint Michael and the Dragon. Spanish (Valencian) Painter, first quarter 15th CE. Tempera on wood, gold around, 41 3/8 x 40 3/4 in.

(105.1 x 103.5 cm). Rogers Fund, 1912 (12.192).
The Metropolitan Museum of Art, New York, NY, U.S.A.
Image copyright © The Metropolitan Museum of Art. Image source: Art Resource, NY

Printed in the United States of America

It was pride that changed angels into devils; it is humility that makes men as angels.

— *Augustine*

The desire of excessive power caused the angels to fall; the desire of knowledge caused men to fall.

— *Francis Bacon*

Man was created a little lower than the angels
and has been getting a little lower ever since.

— Josh Billings

Overview of the Conversation

Some bigger questions...

In and around heaven...

Digging deeper...

Let's get practical...

Wrapping it up...

1

#12

#2

#3

No

Put p. 178 The Lord's Prayer here

How the devil operates...

Since even the saved sin, does that mean the saved are "of Satan"? 168

In what way is the world under Satan's control? 169

The temptation conundrum...

Are you suggesting Satan's power has been curtailed? 171

If Satan was defeated at the cross, why is he still a force to be reckoned with? 173

Are you saying that Satan doesn't tempt us? 176

How are we supposed to understand "the Lord's prayer"? 178

About John's Apocalypse...

What are we meant to understand about Satan from Revelation? 180

Why does Satan figure so prominently in the seven letters? 182

What does Revelation tell us about Satan's ultimate end? 184

The really BIG questions...

Why would God permit Satan to exist and spread his evil? 185

So doesn't that make Satan God's servant? 187

Part Three: Speaking of Demons 191

Making careful distinctions...

Nowhere, then everywhere...

This matter of possession...

Current concerns...

About spiritual warfare...

Preface

Angels, demons, and the devil have fascinated man from the dawn of time. Throughout the centuries, there's been no end to all the speculation, discussion, and debate about these spiritual beings. Even now, contemporary interest in angels is especially keen, as best seen in the mass-marketing of angel figures, angel art, and angel books. The world is awash with wings!

In the bizarre world of the occult, of course, there is also great interest in the darker side. But in contemporary Christian literature, far less attention has been paid to demons and the devil than to angels, except in books dealing with spiritual warfare. The reason, I suspect, is that biblical references to demons and the devil are even more difficult to understand than the many difficult passages relating to angels. Of all the religious topics I have written about, this one has provided the greatest challenge.

To the many friends who have listened to me moan over the past several months, I have been explaining it this way. With most theological issues, there may be, say, fifty core passages that speak directly to the topic under discussion—forty or forty-five of which are fairly straightforward in terms of what most scholars would agree on. Typically, the remaining five-to-ten problematic passages will ultimately be interpreted through the lens of what is known from the clearer forty or forty-five. It doesn't necessarily mean that even the clearer passages will all be interpreted alike. Pre-existing theological mind-sets often become the filter through which one understands the total package. But it does mean that there is more likely to be a greater comfort zone for any and all perspectives. With less effort expended on individual texts, one concentrates on the larger picture.

All of that changes radically when one carefully researches the subject at hand. Staying with our arbitrary figure of fifty core passages, you'd be lucky to find even five or ten straightforward texts on which most scholars agree. The remaining forty or forty-five are all problematic — linguistically, contextually, and theologically. Making life even more difficult, each passage has its own toggle switch. How you flip the switch on each passage will affect how you are likely to flip the switch on other passages, each of which is equally mystifying. "Fog times fog is fog squared!"

By no means, then, do I claim to have resolved all the textual problems related to this topic. Presumptuous indeed is the person who could claim with complete confidence that he has perfectly assembled all the pieces of this elusive puzzle. If challenged on my understanding of any given passage, I'm sure I'd quickly have to capitulate. Consequently, out of all the books I have written, the conclusions in this book are the most tentative I have ever put forward.

Just a word or two in this regard about the approach and format of the book in your hands. I came to this project with as few preconceptions as I have ever had. Indeed, I wrote the book, not to advance any established viewpoint, but to force myself to think seriously about a subject which for a lifetime I had somehow managed to avoid. My aim was to search the Scriptures for any passages which might possibly shed light on the subject and to include each and every one of them in my final manuscript. Unless I have slipped up and overlooked some obscure reference, this work should be a complete compendium of all the relevant texts. Hopefully, this in itself will lend value to the book.

In addition to identifying and considering all the biblical texts, I also did my homework reading what others have said about the subject. With few exceptions, I was surprised at the lack of in-depth discussion of the complete canon. Even the more scholarly books that cover most of the pertinent passages tend to comment on the component "trees" without making any conscious effort to join them all together in a single, comprehensive and cohesive "forest." As helpful as their contribution is for the many difficult passages through which one must navigate, sadly no sharp picture emerges from their work.

Hopefully this background explains why I have chosen the somewhat unusual format of presenting make-believe question-and-answer sessions with Michael the archangel. If anyone should know everything there is to know about angels, demons, and the devil, surely it would be Michael! Importantly for the unique aim of this book, using Michael's voice served to staunch any temptation toward ambiguity or scholarly waffle. I trust you will see this for what it is — merely a literary device.

I suspect that at times you might see my own biases slipping through Michael's lips, not all of which I can vouchsafe would meet his approval. While I certainly hope they *would* (meaning they would be unquestionably biblical and true), I can only say that I've shared my best understanding of the larger theological canvas on which the biblical picture of angels, demons, and the devil is painted. Changing the metaphor, not only must all the pieces of this particular puzzle fit neatly, but — once assembled — they in turn become a "single piece" of a much larger puzzle in which all of the distinct pieces must also fit.

Angels, Demons, and the Devil

Whether we like it or not, our understanding of angels, demons, and the devil cannot help but rub up against whatever theological framework we happen to accept. Should there be noticeable gaps or discrepancies, either we have this topic right and our doctrine wrong, or our doctrine right and this topic wrong. (God forbid that we have *both* of them wrong!) However we come out, the potential benefits are well worth the exercise. Because Scripture itself is unified and cohesive, testing each discreet part of what we have come to believe is a good way of ensuring that we have properly considered every other part.

Regrettably, it would have been unduly intrusive to include discussion of all the factors persuading me to lean one way or the other on any given passage. (Or to explore, for example, all the various views as to when the book of Job was written.) For the most troublesome passages, however, I hope "Michael" has shared enough of his rationale so that you can test his thinking. At times, he and I had quite some discussion about how much he was to say on the matter!

On a technical note, you will soon see that, in keeping with the conversational tone of the book, I have paraphrased virtually all of the scripture quotations, drawing heavily on the New International Version. I have also attempted to highlight any significant differences in translations, such as the King James Version's prolific use of "devil" when "demon" is the more probable sense.

One final caution. Despite what might be suggested by the conversational format, don't expect this work to be a page-turner or thriller. If you're hoping for something like C. S. Lewis' *Screwtape Letters*, I'm afraid you will be disappointed.

Preface

The sole aim in using the format I have chosen is to achieve a coherent narrative which best reflects the scores of pertinent biblical texts on the subjects at hand. Call me linear. It's truth I'm after, not existential musings. So if the book fails to grip you, at least let it grasp you.

In the end, my prayer for this book is that it will stir renewed consideration of an area of great biblical importance that too often has been either wholly ignored or badly mangled. If there are things that even angels have longed to look into, as Peter suggests, I regret having waited so long to return the favor.

F. LaGard Smith

Part One

Speaking of Angels

Man is neither angel nor beast; and the misfortune is
that he who would act the angel acts the beast.

— Blaise Pascal

Permit me to introduce myself. I'm Michael, an angel of God. I
understand you have questions about heavenly beings...and
about the spiritual forces of darkness. You are not alone, of
course. Over the centuries virtually everyone has wondered
about us angels, and the demons as well. More especially
about the Evil One. As you can appreciate, there are limits to
what I can share with you, not the least being what I am
strictly forbidden to disclose. In time, you will know all that
we angels know, and even future events that we ourselves are
curious about.[1]

For the moment, the greater problem is conveying that which
I'm authorized to discuss in a way you can understand.

---

1. 1 Peter 1:12

Angels, Demons, and the Devil

Already, the difficulty in bridging the gap between the spiritual and physical realms has caused much confusion. Graphic images intended to awaken earthly resonance with "the other world," as you speak of it, have often taken on a greater significance than the transcendent reality those images were intended to signify. That was always a risk, but there was no other way to resolve the problem if there was to be a temporal, physical cosmos existing apart from the heavenlies.

You already may have considered the irony of the conundrum — that God set man in a material world in part to draw man, by every parable of nature, away from the blinding materiality of a material world! Had that enigma not been explained to us, we ourselves would still be mystified. One day, you too shall marvel at this mystery revealed.

Yet you should not think that a wholly spiritual heaven is without its own perplexities. Even with no gap between the heavenly realm and some parallel physical universe, it is still possible to worship created things rather than the Creator himself. About that, we can talk more later. Suffice it to say for the moment that there is no easy way to stretch your finite mind around the sublimely infinite in order fully to grasp that sphere. No matter how much you might wish to move beyond what might be considered an infantile understanding toward a more mature insight, your humanity is necessarily child-like.

Consider then my conversations to be in the nature of a parent attempting to explain the unexplainable to questioning children filled with more curiosity than perception. (Even now I have resorted to a parable!) So with this feeble disclaimer on the table, I will do my best to answer your many questions.

*W*hat is your role as an archangel? I'm tempted to say that it's doing whatever onerous task the Lord graciously refuses to impose on any other celestials! Certainly, being a chief among angels is not to be understood as a position of greater honor, only greater responsibility.[2] One of my primary responsibilities, for example, was to protect Israel from those who sought to destroy her.[3] Frankly, that was always the easier part. The more difficult challenge was protecting Israel from herself—a task at which, as you undoubtedly know, I was not always successful. The seductive idolatry championed by the Evil One and his rebellious angels lured Israel away from God time and again.

Indeed the matter of idolatry was at the heart of my dispute with the Evil One over Moses' body.[4] After Moses had been privileged to view the promised land from the heights of Mount Nebo and came back down into Moab to die as the Lord had determined, I was sent to bury Moses' body. Having strict instructions to hide the body secretly, I was carrying it by stealth to a site I had chosen in the valley opposite Beth Peor when suddenly Satan appeared from the Abyss. I hadn't seen him since the Great Uprising and his fall from heaven. Satan was incensed that so great a servant of God was going to be buried secretly as if in ignominy. Moses deserved an elaborate monument befitting his stature, he said. I was not fooled in the least by the Evil One's pretended concern for Moses' legacy. Satan was opposed to all that Moses represented: obedience to law, purity, holiness, and godly reverence.

So why his pretense? Because the Evil One was well aware of Israel's weakness for idolatry. Left to him, Moses' elaborate

---

2. Daniel 10:13
3. Daniel 10:21;12:1
4. Jude 1:9; Deuteronomy 34:5-6

burial site would have become a place of pilgrim veneration and, in time, yet one more idol to be worshiped. What unspeakable irony it would have been to desecrate the memory of Israel's great lawgiver by turning his tomb into a high holy place condemned by the very law Moses had given! "May the Holy One rebuke you!" I said in utter outrage, and abruptly ordered him back into the Abyss where he belonged.

But I digress. Many have thought that my very name somehow implies a likeness to God not far removed from the Messiah himself. In that they are gravely mistaken regarding both form and function. As a created being, I am not to be compared with the eternal Son of God, the incarnate Messiah Christ. Nor am I in a position of divine authority, but simply a willing servant.

While my role as an archangel is infinitely gratifying and rewarding, at times the challenges which must be shouldered are daunting. Never was that more true than on the occasion to which I briefly alluded — the internecine warfare that ripped apart heaven's tranquility.[5] I'll be happy to speak more about that as we move along, but simply to say at this point that one would not likely apply to be an archangel if he knew the demands of the office. Indeed, the Evil One's lust for position and power — the seminal cause of the conflict — evidenced a woeful lack of understanding about the burdens of high office.

I confess I do look forward to that day when the Lord will return to earth in glory to judge the living and the dead. I myself do not know the time,[6] but I've been told that I will have the great privilege of announcing the Lord's coming with a

---

5. Revelation 12:7-9
6. Matthew 24:36; Mark 13:32

trumpet call, as it were, and with a booming voice to be heard by the most distant stars.[7] What a thrill that will be! What a Day that will be!

*W*hat can you say about Gabriel? I'm glad you asked, especially since (speaking of trumpet calls and that great gettin'-up morning) everyone seems to talk about nothing but Gabriel blowing his horn! Actually, Gabriel and I are like right and left hands working together. There was the time, for instance, when Gabriel needed backup on his mission to convince Cyrus to issue the decree for the Jews to return to Jerusalem after their seventy-year exile. Because this matter touched directly on the nation with which I was specially entrusted, I was happy to join with Gabriel to achieve that beneficent result. Cyrus had no natural reason to aid the Jews, so softening his heart in keeping with God's sovereign plan was a struggle.[8]

Gabriel and I also worked together during the reign of Darius the Mede, who was to play a crucial role especially in issuing a decree proclaiming reverence for God in the wake of our delivering Daniel from the den of lions.[9] Afterwards, Gabriel would "do business" with that mighty prince of Greece, Alexander the Great. Establishing Alexander's reign would pave the way for the coming kingdom of the Messiah, particularly in extending the reach of the Greek language which would become such an effective vehicle for propagating the good news about Christ.

---

7. 1 Thessalonians 4:16
8. 2 Chronicles 36:22-23; Ezra 1:1-4; Daniel 10:12-21
9. Daniel 6:1-27; 9:1-2; 10:20-11:1

As he reminds me good-naturedly, Gabriel has always gotten all the "Big Announcement" assignments. For instance, who got to explain that cryptic vision to Daniel as he sat beside the Ulai Canal; and later to tell him of the "seventy sevens"?[10] Gabriel! And who was privileged to announce to Zechariah that he and Elizabeth would soon conceive John?[11] Gabriel, of course! And then—honor of all honors—again it was Gabriel whom God called to break the wonderful news to Mary about the coming Christ child who would issue forth from her womb by the Holy Spirit.[12] You must ask Gabriel about Mary's beautiful spirit when she received the incredible news that she would become pregnant despite being a virgin. He can also tell you about Joseph's understandable incredulity after he appeared to him in a dream to tell him his betrothed was about to become mysteriously pregnant![13]

And who do you suppose brought the glorious announcement of Jesus' birth to the shepherds in the field?[14] You guessed it! And who appeared in Joseph's dreams to warn him to flee into Egypt; then later appeared to say the coast was clear for their return to Israel?[15] Right again! If Gabriel really did have a horn, he'd certainly have every reason to go around tooting it!

*D*o angels really have wings? Why is this always one of the first questions? Well, let me quickly dispel the myth of angel wings. I'm sorry to burst any bubbles, but we do not, in fact, have wings. I suppose it's not

---

10. Daniel 8:1-27; 9:20-27
11. Luke 1:8-20
12. Luke 1:26-38
13. Matthew 1:18-25; Luke 2:21
14. Luke 2:8-14
15. Matthew 2:13; 2:19-20

surprising that people would imagine us with wings, especially given the winged cherubim in the tabernacle and temple,[16] and the vivid descriptions of various heavenly creatures
(like those with four or six wings) particularly in the visions to
Isaiah, Ezekiel, and John.[17] I'm always amazed that wings have
become so widely associated with angels. The same visions
also speak of whirring wheels, but somehow wheels haven't
caught on in all the "angel art" you see.

Not only are we wingless, we don't exactly "fly" in any real
sense of the word. Yes, I know that in his magnificent throne vision Isaiah describes seraphs having six wings, two of which
were for "flying;" and how one of the seraphs "flew" to him
with a burning coal from the altar.[18] Similarly, in his majestic
Apocalypse John sees "an angel flying in midair," just as he had
seen an eagle "flying in midair."[19] But one must not take those
visions literally, only the seriousness of the message those figurative images were meant to convey. Indeed, "flying" would be
a limitation on the immediacy with which we can move within
heaven, and between heaven and earth. In our realm of existence, the rules of time and space simply don't apply.

There was that occasion, for instance, when Daniel was in
prayer and suddenly Gabriel appeared, ready to answer the
prayer Daniel had not yet even finished. Just how quick is
that! No wonder Daniel speaks in terms of "swift flight."[20] But
Gabriel was not simply faster than a speeding bullet, he was
faster than the word *flight* can begin to conjure. Words

---

16. Exodus 25:17-22; 37:1-9; Numbers 7:89; 1 Chronicles 28:18;
    2 Chronicles 3:10-13; 5:7-8; 1 Kings 6:23-28; 7:29, 36; 8:6-7
17. Isaiah 6:1-7; Ezekiel 1:4-25; 3:12-13; 9:3; 10:1-22; 11:22;
    Revelation 4:7-8
18. Isaiah 6:1-7
19. Revelation 8:13; 14:6
20. Daniel 9:20-23

depicting *flight* and *flying* serve to heighten your appreciation for a transcendent reality you otherwise couldn't begin to comprehend, and even about God and his incomparable glory. Think, for example, of David's graphic depiction of God coming to his rescue when he was surrounded by the enemy and very nearly at the point of death. David imagines God hearing his cry for help and immediately "flying" down from heaven mounted on cherubs and appearing on the wings of the wind.[21] Naturally, God wasn't literally *flying*. While David's poetic picture was not meant to reflect reality, the point is that David's divine rescue was!

First seen on some of the ancient Egyptian and Babylonian demi-gods, "angel wings" became absolutely indispensable during Medieval times, the golden age of angel mythology. It seems that every angel ever painted or sculpted (including the anonymous, 15th century painting of me on the front cover of this book) was depicted with those dreadful wings! (Look closely, and you'll see that the artist's wings were modeled after the largest birds around — like swans, geese, and storks. Strictly from an anatomical standpoint, those paltry wings would not be proportionally large enough for "human-like angels"!) But don't be fooled by all that silliness. We definitely don't have wings, and — despite all the rumors — neither will you in heaven.

*a*re cherubs and seraphs truly celestial beings? Given what I've just said about angels not literally having wings, I see where you're coming from. But, yes, they are definitely real...at least if we all understand what we're talking about. Certainly there is a genuine reality *behind* the

---

21. Psalm 18:10; 2 Samuel 22:11

names and colorful images. The terms *cherub* and *seraph* generically describe angels having a special role and function in the heavenly panoply. Yet you should not hastily assume, as do many, that there is some kind of corporate-ladder hierarchy among the heavenly beings such as you might expect with human organizations and government. Cherubs and seraphs are no more "at the top" of the celestial ladder than, say, an archangel.

Just as God has given some within the church to be apostles, prophets, teachers, and recipients of various kinds of gifts, all for the edification of the body, so too God has also given to his heavenly host a variety of gifts and responsibilities — all for the fulfillment of his eternal will. Some of these gifts pertain specifically to "thrones," "dominions," "principalities," and "powers," but it would be hard for you to grasp all of that fully until you're on the other side. What's important is that, just as no gift within the church is more important to the body than any other, no angelic role — not even the most powerful — is intrinsically superior to any other.

As you may already know, the term *seraph*, or plurally *seraphim*, (denoting a "burning" or "flame," not unlike the angelic "chariots of fire" Elisha saw[22]) is found only in Isaiah's inaugural vision.[23] Use of that term to describe the angels whom God sent to equip Isaiah for his prophetic mission gives special emphasis to the purifying fire which they brought for his unclean lips. (However, just to confuse you further, at times the angels referred to as *cherubs* are no less associated with burning coal and fire.[24]) One should not think that the seraphim were in form or in character a distinct, unique kind

---

22. 2 Kings 6:17
23. Isaiah 6:1-7
24. Ezekiel 10:1-8

of heavenly being. The term speaks only to how these particular angels were specially presented in Isaiah's vision. To draw an analogy from human experience, the same woman might be a mother, daughter, homemaker, or businesswoman—all depending upon the given context. So when it comes to the various roles and fantastic visionary descriptions of angels, don't be tempted to make more of the term *seraph* than was ever intended on this one occasion.

It is likewise true of cherubs, whose name, meaning "near ones," speaks of those angels called for special duty at God's right hand to bring his presence to bear wherever and whenever needed. Never was that divine presence needed more than when man first presumed to disobey God by eating from the forbidden tree. Since the first couple had already decided it would be desirable to be their own arbiter of good and evil, God was not about to let them once again self-destruct in an even more disastrous way. So as Adam and Eve were being ushered out of the pristine Garden into a toilsome and painful world, you may recall mention of cherubs being placed on the east side of the Garden (along with a flaming sword flashing back and forth) to guard against any access to the tree of life.[25]

Incidentally, there's no use going in search of Eden's famed Garden these days, or the tree of life, or the cherubs standing guard. For all the historical reality of your forebears and their notorious sin, one should not concentrate overly much on the antediluvian geography or archeology of the Creation account revealed to Moses. Accept its fundamental truth (particularly in contrast to counterfeit materialist versions of man's origin), but focus more on its meaning.

---

25. Genesis 3:24

In other words, think less of some discoverable "tree" (as if you could see it or touch it) and more about the distinction it represents between the eternal nature that only God can have and, by contrast, man's merely prospective immortality. It is *human presumptiveness* that God has assigned his cherub angels to guard against. How could it be either to God's glory or to man's good that anyone should believe man to be eternal as God is eternal? Yet, because even in your generation there are some New Age types and others who claim man is eternal, still today cherubs from the Throne of God prevent such blasphemy from fully taking root throughout the world.

To say "God's cherubs" is really to speak of the divine presence which they represent, whether on the "east side of the Garden" or elsewhere. Especially was that the case with the cherubs in the tabernacle and temple...at least in a manner of speaking. What's interesting from your perspective is that you see cherubs spoken of on a number of different levels, in some cases almost simultaneously. In the ancient tabernacle and later temple, for example, God specifically directed that there should be "cherubim" placed above the mercy seat in front of the Holy of Holies.[26] No one in either heaven or earth suggests that these handsomely crafted "cherubim" are *real* cherubs. Those who believe them to be sculptures of what real cherubs actually look like, have misunderstood altogether the spiritual nature of cherubs, which is to say *angels*.

The point of having carved and gilded cherubs at the very seat of Israel's worship was to represent God's personal presence among his people. Where in the tabernacle did Moses hear God speaking? From *between the two cherubim* above the atonement

26. Exodus 25:17-22; 37:1-9; Numbers 7:89; 1 Chronicles 28:18;
    2 Chronicles 3:10-13; 5:7-8; 1 Kings 6:23-28; 7:29, 36; 8:6-7

cover on the ark of the Testimony.[27] Even when God no longer spoke so directly to Moses' successors, the symbolism of God's presence in the house of God remained.[28] Indeed, the graphic images of cherubs (along with lions, bulls, and palm trees) carved into the bronze stands in Solomon's temple[29] (as well as throughout the temple described in Ezekiel's "great temple vision"[30]) was to be a reminder that God's presence filled not only that house of worship but the whole of nature.

All of which has its own implications for you as well. Do you see a flower? In the sense we're now speaking of, that glorious flower is a "cherub" of God announcing his divine presence. Do you see a rainbow, or forest, or cloud, or distant twinkling star? They, too, are all God's "cherubs" so that he might come into your presence and speak to you. In the simplest possible way, then, "cherubs" can refer to anything that represents God's presence among you. But it gets rather more complicated after that!

For Ezekiel, seeing cherubs became so mind-boggling that at one point he sat by the Kebar River completely overwhelmed for seven days.[31] You'll undoubtedly recall his exciting exile visions — first, of the "four living creatures" with the four faces and four wings,[32] then later his stirring temple vision with its fascinating "cherubim" and their "whirring wheels."[33] As Ezekiel stands beside the altar in the vision, suddenly the glory of the Lord rises above the cherubim. Just when you

---

27. Numbers 7:89
28. 1 Samuel 4:4; 2 Samuel 6:2; 1 Chronicles 13:6; 2 Kings 19:15; Isaiah 37:16; Psalm 80:1; 99:1
29. 1 Kings 7:27-37
30. Ezekiel 41:17-20
31. Ezekiel 3:15
32. Ezekiel 1:1-25
33. Ezekiel 8:1-11:25

might assume he's talking simply about the two magnificent gilded cherubs over the mercy seat where God's glory normally rested, Ezekiel begins to describe "the wheels beneath the cherubim," which has nothing to do with those two temple cherubs. In fact, Ezekiel explains that these "cherubim" are the "four living creatures" he had seen in his earlier vision—the four-faced creatures with the four wings and intersecting wheels.[34]

At which point it must become all the more fascinating for you, as you read that each of these cherubs had four faces: one of an eagle, one of a lion, one of a man, and *one of a cherub!*[35] If you're confused as to how that works, all I can tell you is that the vision is not unlike the bizarre "film productions" you see in your dreams, which sometimes are seemingly real in every detail but at other times are completely fantastic.

We've moved now from a pair of crafted cherubs above the mercy seat (representing God's presence in worship) to fantastically-described cherubs in Ezekiel's vision (representing God's presence in judgment on Israel), and full-circle back to the cherubs stationed protectively on the east side of the Garden (representing God's presence in unchallenged eternal glory). So are cherubs *real*? As you can see, it depends upon which "cherubs" you're asking about! But, yes, God does indeed have cherub angels specially designated to convey his divine presence to man. If sometimes they are visually represented as carved wood or fantastical dream-like creatures, even so these angels of God are every bit as real as you and I.

---

34. Ezekiel 10:20
35. Ezekiel 10:14

Far more important, the *message* they bring is real! People who become obsessed with fanciful attempts to identify every detail of the wings and faces and intersecting wheels of the cherubs (especially with the end-times in view) are not only wasting their time but missing the whole point of the exercise. The message accompanying the "four living creatures" in particular was all about God's judgment against Israel's unfaithful idolatry; about unchecked bloodshed in the streets; and about shameful injustice to the poor and oppressed. If you want to make some modern-day applications (and you *must*), God's cherubs are not speaking to you about the *end times* but *your own time*. God's judgment is not just past and future but *present*!

Draw us a picture...

So what *do* angels look like? I can appreciate that you find it difficult to picture us without wings and the almost human-like features and clothing so much a part of angel art. (It's not just the grotesque wings. In every respect that painting of me on the front cover couldn't be a sillier depiction!) Would you expect God himself to have wings and clothes and human features? Granted, God is often described in Scripture as having various human attributes, such as a face, arms, hands, and a heart. But except for the incarnate Christ, these personifications were never meant to be taken literally. The point is that we angels do not have what you would call *physical* form of any kind. As spirit beings, we have only *spiritual* form.[36] It won't be easy, but try to wrap your mind around the idea of *matterless form* without it actually being *formless*!

---

36. Psalm 104:4; Hebrews 1:7

Speaking of Angels

Having said that we are "matterless," I should make one thing perfectly clear. We are not matterless because there's anything bad about physical matter. Your much-celebrated philosopher Plato was extraordinarily bright, but he was terribly wrong to assume that physical matter is fundamentally evil and best escaped if at all possible. What in the world was he thinking? God *created* physical matter, and deemed it *very good*! So heaven is certainly not about escaping an evil physical world. To the contrary, a "very good" physical world is God's ingenious "stepping stone" to a non-physical (matterless) realm that is even better. As in good, better, and *best*!

On reflection, I honestly don't know what's more disturbing: Plato's wrong-headed idea about physical matter, or those who try to counter Plato by going to the opposite extreme, insisting that, at the Resurrection, the bodies of the righteous will be merely non-mortal replicas of their own earthly, physical bodies and virtually the same as Jesus' resurrected body. I fully appreciate the conundrum of Jesus' resurrected body—able to be touched, able to eat fish ("I am not a ghost!"), and yet also able to walk through bolted doors. But I assure you that when Jesus ascended back into heaven, his flesh-and-blood physical body (necessary to convince the world that resurrection is real) was ingloriously shed along the way. When people utter such nonsense as "the *human* Jesus is now in heaven," don't you believe it. There is no human hunger for fish in heaven, and certainly no fish! Nor, to be frank, any human need for eliminating waste—all of which Jesus shared as part of the human experience during his sojurn on earth.

Those who speak derisively of "disembodied souls floating around in heaven" have no idea what they're talking about. Not even we angels are "disembodied"! The questing folks should be asking isn't whether the righteous will have bodies in heaven (that's a given!). The only issue is *what kind of bodies they will be*. Will they be recognizable as the bodies you now have, or will they be as indescribably different as a butterfly from the larva out of which it emerges?

But before we speak too much of heaven, we should take a passing glance at the crucial matter of the intermediate state of the dead prior to Resurrection. At the point where one's fleshly body has been buried or cremated, and before being re-clothed with one's resurrection body, what can one be other than a "disembodied soul"? Not to mention the Lord's own mind-boggling *incarnation* with its necessary implication that, *in heaven prior to his birth in Bethlehem,* Christ obviously had no flesh-and-blood physical body, nor even the intermediate "showcase" body witnessed by so many people following his resurrection from the tomb.

None of which is to say that we angels are "disembodied souls," only that, while you might reasonably assume from an earthly perspective that we are disembodied spirits, in truth we are not exactly "disembodied." It's just that our celestial forms are "bodies" unlike any "bodies" you can possibly imagine. You may recall the apostle Paul's attempt to distinguish post-resurrection spiritual "bodies" from the physical, flesh-and-blood bodies in which you now exist.[37] Until you yourself see such a "body" — or more properly *experience* such a radically different heavenly form — you will never come close to grasping its substance or appearance. (Could any curious infant in the womb possibly imagine life outside the womb?)

The one mistake you must not make is in thinking that our spirits are just kind of "floating around" out there somewhere.

---

37. 1 Corinthians 15:35-58

Like any other "bodies," our is a definable form, only quite fantastic and—if I may say so—spectacularly luminous compared with yours! Not to mention unbelievably mobile, and capable of doing amazing things you could never imagine. One day you'll see. The word going around heaven is that your resurrection body will be altogether as interesting as ours!

The good news for us is that, having spiritual rather than physical bodies, we don't get hungry, or have sexual desires, or grow tired, or need sleep, or experience disease, old age, or death.[38] I say "good news," because among the many other advantages of not having physical bodies is that we don't have to deal with any temptations associated with corporeal human experience. Gluttony? Not a problem. Lust? We couldn't be bothered. The kind of covetousness that would lead to theft? What would there be in heaven for us to steal! Yet that's not to say that we are incapable of sin. Far from it. Ask me later about celestial pride, envy, jealousy, and heavenly hatred. That's a different story altogether!

*H*ow would you describe an angel? You may not realize it, but that's somewhat of a trick question. If you're speaking of *heavenly* angels, there is much of interest to tell you. But because the word *angel* describes *any messenger*, whether divine or human, it is proper to speak even of human messengers as "angels," no matter how mundane and non-spiritual the message. When a coach sends a player onto the field with instructions for his teammates, that player would never guess it to be so, but all 250 muscle-pulsing pounds of him is an angel! When a teacher brings words of

---

38. Luke 20:35-36

explanation to a class full of students, the teacher — no matter how brutally tough a grader — is an angel. Ambassadors and couriers are certainly "angels." And radio announcers and television presenters are angels, whatever their particular slant on the news. As are gospel preachers, instructive parents, and even stern-faced policemen, who in their own maddening, unwelcome way sometimes help you "get the message"! The *form* of all these human "angels" is readily apparent, especially those wearing uniforms with badges!

You will have read of many human messengers in the Bible. Remember when Jezebel sent a messenger to threaten Elijah? The word "messenger" there actually means "angel."[39] Same with David sending messengers ("angels") to the men of Jabesh Gilead.[40] And the same again with John's disciples whom John sent to question Jesus.[41] By some irony, John the forerunner of Christ (whom you call "John the Baptist" because he immersed his disciples in the Jordan), was himself an "angel" or "messenger."[42] In that same sense, when God "sent his angel" to deliver Israel out of Egypt, he not only showed his divine power and presence through heavenly angels but sent Moses as Israel's human "angel" to deliver God's emancipating messages to Pharaoh.[43]

Haggai the prophet was also said to be a "messenger," from the root word, *mal'akh*, meaning "angel."[44] In fact, being a messenger was the primary role of prophets, serving as God's

39. 1 Kings 19:2. See also: Luke 9:52; 2 Corinthians 12:7; Galatians 4:14; James 2:25
40. 2 Samuel 2:5
41. Luke 7:24
42. Malachi 3:1; Mark 1:2
43. Numbers 20:16
44. Haggai 1:13

"angels" to bring words of rebuke or encouragement from above. (Consider, for example, that "man of God" who brought the bad news of God's judgment against Eli.[45]) Priests, too, were "angels" or "messengers" when they instructed the people about God's will.[46] (So reports the prophet Malachi, whose very name means "angel"!) And then there are those ministering (message-giving) "angels" of the seven churches in Asia, to whom John was commissioned to deliver all those heavy rebukes from the Lord.[47] (John wasn't being sent by one heavenly angel to bring the Lord's message to another *heavenly* angel!) To think that all "angels" are celestial beings is seriously to miss the message!

In fact, "messenger angels" may at times even be inanimate, as when God causes winds and fire to bring about his judgment or blessing.[48] Next time you hear a howling wind, it might give you cause for pause!

*I*n what form do angels appear on earth? Sorry. I know that's what you were *really* asking in your previous question, but I simply had to clarify some things before moving on. Let me begin with just a quick word of caution. If ever you hear someone claim to have seen one of us, check out how they describe us. For openers, if they mention wings, they're operating in fantasyland. And if they paint a vivid picture of phosphorescent spirits looking like they just stepped out of a spaceship, again, forget it.

---

45. 1 Samuel 2:27-36
46. Malachi 2:7
47. Revelation 1:20; 2:1, 8, 12, 18; 3:1, 7, 14
48. Psalm 104:4 (Note a rather different connotation in KJV.)

Naturally, no one in the first century would have thought in terms of spaceships, but nobody could have missed the startling brilliance of the angel who rolled back the stone at Jesus' tomb. It caused the guards such a fright that they passed out cold![49] And just imagine the look on the faces of the women approaching Jesus' tomb when they were suddenly confronted by the same angel (at that point appearing as a more normal-looking "young man," yet still wearing a striking white robe), and thereafter were surprised by two other men whose clothes shimmered like lightning![50] In case you've ever wondered how those who were watching Stephen's Sanhedrin defense concluded his soon-to-be-martyred face was "like the face of an angel," there had been enough extraordinary appearances for striking images of that kind to emerge in the imaginations of the common man.[51]

However, our usual *modus operandi* is to appear completely normal, as if we are just as human as you are. Remember when Samuel instructed Saul to meet "two men" near Rachel's tomb, and then "three men" at the great tree of Tabor?[52] Saul didn't know it, but these "men" were angels sent to give him reassurance that God was calling him to be Israel's first king.

Maybe our usual normalcy will come as a disappointment to you, but it also suggests something you may never have thought about. Have you ever considered that Jesus was not the only heavenly being to be manifest on earth in human form? Yet, be ever so careful here. The unique incarnation of Jesus of Nazareth is distinct in that he, and only he, was *God* in flesh. And was born of a woman; and was a child who grew

---

49. Matthew 28:2-4
50. Matthew 28:5-7; Mark 16:5-7; Luke 24:4-8
51. Acts 6:15
52. 1 Samuel 10:1-4

into maturity; and died in the flesh. We angels are *not* God.
Nor have we ever experienced human birth or death, or developed physically from childhood into manhood. Huge difference that!

It's all the more remarkable, then, that Jesus himself was an "angel" in the sense we just talked about—as the ultimate Messenger of divine truth and wisdom. Who could miss his "angelic" mission when he asserts that he was sent from the Father[53] and speaks only what he is commanded to say by the Father![54] (In fact, the Son of God, before he was the incarnate Jesus, appeared on earth much like other angels—sometimes in flaming brilliance—compared to the man from Nazareth walking on the earth in the first century. Stay tuned on that one!)

Returning to your original question, one of the reasons there's so much confusion about our "physical" appearance (whether on earth or in heaven) is the way we are depicted in various visions—say, to Ezekiel or Daniel or the apostle John. But those *visionary depictions* are not at all how we have appeared in our "human" visitations. Visions are surreal, dream-like fantasies. Their digitally-enhanced imagery was never meant to be taken as real, only as conveying the underlying truths those images were intended to project.

So don't be sidetracked when Ezekiel and Daniel relate their visions about "the man clothed in linen" whose body was like crysolite, with a face like lightning and eyes like flaming torches; his arms and legs like burnished bronze, and his voice sounding like a multitude.[55] Fantasy descriptions like that are

---

53. John 8:16, 18, 42
54. John 12:49-50; 14:24
55. Ezekiel 9:1-10:8; Daniel 10:4-11:1; 12:5-12

not meant to be taken literally, as if that's what angels look like on either side of the Great Divide. Especially beware of reading too much into *any* apocalyptic images, such as those which John relates in his Revelation.[56]

When we celestial beings show up in your world for real, we instantly adapt to your earthly environment. To use your word, we *morph*. Now you see us, now you don't. Now you *don't* see us, now you *do*! And when you do, your could never pick us out of a lineup as being any different from anybody else. Abraham, for example, didn't have a clue at first. His unannounced guests even ate in his presence.[57] Nor did those perverted Sodomites have any idea who they were lusting after. The first they knew that those two "visitors to Sodom" were not the average tourists they assumed them to be was when those "men" struck them blind![58]

Does this explain how it is possible for you to entertain angels without knowing it, thinking they are mere strangers in need of hospitality?[59] Once you forget about the proverbial wings and shimmering robes, angels will become far more real to you. And that would be a good thing!

*I*f we see angels in our dreams, are they real? I guarantee you would know! You wouldn't have to wonder whether you were just imagining things. Did any of the ancients who encountered angels in dreams ever have to think twice about whether it was a normal dream or a truly extraordinary one? When you consider the dreams like those given

---

56. Revelation 4:6-8
57. Genesis 18:1-8
58. Genesis 19:1-11
59. Hebrews 13:2

to, say, Jacob and Mary's betrothed, Joseph, you know that they weren't just an ordinary dream! In those dreams, there were *real* angels speaking *real* words with *real* meaning for *real* circumstances.[60] At times, there were dreamlike visions that suddenly gave way to reality, as was the case with Peter when the angel of his "vision" didn't just disappear, but *left!*[61]

Most important of all, if it's a word from the Lord you're wanting to hear, don't wait for an angel to appear. Dig into his Word! That's your message for today, your "angel," your clearest possible vision from God.

*H*ow do you explain the many "angel sightings"? Discounting any stories where the angels supposedly had wings (your first clue that something's wrong), the next question to be asked is whether anyone near the sighting was so overwhelmed with awe that they either fell to their knees or fled in horror. Either we angels are indistinguishable from ordinary people, or — when not in human disguise — are downright fearsome and frightening! Not many of the popular "angel sightings" can compare with those scenes of sheer terror you read about in your Bible, can they?

Which is not to say that we angels can't be a source of comfort, particularly to those who are about to cross to the other side. If even our *perceived* presence is a comfort to the dying, that's a good thing. We find it a blessing just knowing that believers appreciate a spiritual dimension that others so easily dismiss as pure fantasy.

---

60. Matthew 2:13, 19; Genesis 31:10-13
61. Acts 10:1-8

Angels, Demons, and the Devil

By contrast, when folks tell of seeing their deceased loved ones at the foot of the bed, you can rest assured it's neither the spirits of their loved ones nor us angels. Nor are UFO's or all those other strange lights flashing in the skies manifestations of celestial beings; nor those ghostly images everyone talks about. The plain fact is that one sometimes "sees" what one *wants* to see. But how often do these observers tell of the *message* they were given? After all, that's our primary role when commissioned to come to earth—to say something important, not just to dazzle or performs tricks.

In truth, most "angel sightings" don't pretend to describe someone or something that is seen, but something that has happened—something quite extraordinary which is attributed to us in some way. There's the young boy, for instance, who is walking along a loose board. Just as it begins to tip, inexplicably the board begins to tip the other way as though being pushed down by a hand. Suddenly, the "only explanation" is an angel doing it. Or maybe it's the woman being attacked by a tiger who prays to God and suddenly the tiger breaks off and runs away. Just had to be an angel rescuer, didn't it?

Yet if that's the kind of "sightings" you're asking about, what is to be said of all the other strange coincidences that take place moment to moment throughout the world to which no claim is made of an angel sighting? Naturally, we'd be happy to take credit for any good that might happen, but you should view with caution claims that would turn every unusual phenomenon into an "angel sighting."

The irony of supposed angel sightings is that they often come from some of the least religious people around. Folks who wouldn't bend a knee in prayer to the sovereign God of the universe frequently take great comfort and delight in angels.

Speaking of Angels

By popular perception, we are viewed as higher beings who can be of supernatural aid to mere mortals, but without the onerous downside of a God who demands strict obedience or threatens divine punishment for disobedience. "Benevolent angels" are tailor-made for those who want all the benefits but none of the burdens of spirituality. What these secular spiritualists forget is that one of our most important duties is bringing God's justice to bear against the ungodly![62]

Then again, there are some deeply religious, even "churched," people out there who claim to see us angels behind every rock and tree—and love to tell about it. So much so that (God forbid!) we virtually become objects of worship. Angelolatry is not far removed from idolatry, in which creatures are elevated above the Creator. And I'm not just talking here about elevating angels or some carved wooden idol over the very God who made them both. I'm talking about the people, themselves, who are doing the elevating. By presumptuously bypassing God through either idols or angels, in effect they're elevating *themselves* over God! All the while, they take delight in their false humility, thinking how spiritual they are and going into great detail about the angels they've seen. Let no one be fooled. It's not humility that's driving these imaginations, but puffed up pride![63]

What you must understand is that we are not "on call" for those who simply want to see us. Nor do we appear only to those who believe in us and not to those who dismiss us altogether. Nor must we appear at all in order to do behind the scenes what God asks us to do. Nor, most importantly, does God invariably work through us indirectly as opposed to working directly through his Holy Spirit.

---

62. Acts 12:19-23
63. Colossians 2:18

I can't begin to tell you how important this is. Until the coming of the Holy Spirit after the ascension of Christ, we angels played an active role in bringing about God's eternal plan for mankind. Since that time, our task on earth has been reduced considerably. In the hearts of Christ's true followers, it is the Holy Spirit who is now actively working to produce fruits of the Spirit leading to their sanctification. Although the outward fruits are clearly visible, the Spirit's inner working is quite invisible. It's a new age—which, incidentally, couldn't be farther from today's "New Age" with its fanciful angels speaking to the gullible through enlightened mediums and clairvoyants about past lives, out-of-body experiences, tunnels of light, and at-one-ment with God—a God who turns out to be none other than the New Age believer herself!

In this present era of the Spirit, it is less likely than ever that anyone will have a genuine "angel sighting." No need to call anyone a liar. It's simply a matter of how data is interpreted. That which is subjectively (even sincerely) believed is not always that which is objectively true. Seeing us is not important. What's important is believing that we continue to play a significant role in the invisible sphere intimately intertwined with the visible world in which you live.

*a*re you upset when mortals worship angels? I'll say! We may be called "gods" by many, but we are *not* God![64] And even though we may legitimately be called "holy ones," we are not the *Holy One*![65] That we should in the least be elevated to deity status is unthinkable. Remember when the apostle John confessed—not once, but twice—to

---

64. Psalm 138:1
65. Daniel 4:13, 17, 23

bowing down in worship before the angel he saw in his vision? The angel was quick to respond: "Don't do that! Only God is to be worshiped!"[66] Why else mention it twice but to drive home the point?

Paul was right to remind the disciples in Colosse of the crucial distinction between the Creator and his creatures. As he pointed out, Christ is the image of God and the one through whom all things, visible and invisible, were created.[67] Since "all creation" would include us, what could be more inappropriate than worshiping us?[68] Or venerating us? Or even praying *to* us or *through* us! Where in the Scriptures do you find any hint that we are to be the object of your prayers?

If ever there were any doubt about the worship of angels, the writer of Hebrews should have settled the question once and for all. Have you considered his powerful argument? It is Christ alone who is to be worshiped, he reasons, because Christ is superior to us angels in every respect.[69] To begin with, God calls Christ his Son in a way he has never once called any of us his "Son," as in *the one and only Son*. And when he brought his Son into the world, the decree went out, "Command all my angels to worship him" — which we did (and *do*), gladly and joyfully.[70] Nor to any of us angels has God ever said, "Sit at my right hand." We are but Christ's ministers and servants. It is not we, but Christ, to whom the world to come will be in subjection. So why would anyone dare worship us?

---

66. Revelation 19:9-10; 22:8-9
67. Colossians 1:15-20
68. Romans 1:24-25
69. Hebrews 1:4-2:18
70. Deuteronomy 32:43 (Septuagint)

*D*id angels really have sex with humans? Oh, so you've heard about the age-old "Nephilim debate" arising out of the Genesis account of the "sons of God" who married the "daughters of men."[71] This isn't my favorite question, as you can imagine, but I suppose there's no way around it.

Let me caution you even before we get started that we need to be careful here regarding the word *Nephilim*, which simply means "giant." Much confusion has been engendered by various Scripture translations which—by using *Nephilim* rather than *giant*—give the false impression that the "Nephilim" were some distinct class of giants, as if a race or clan all their own. That's simply not the case. (Indeed, the word *giant* doesn't even necessarily speak of those who were enormous in physical stature, but also of persons of great intellect, knowledge, or power.)

One could be forgiven, of course, for thinking that Moses' reference to "sons of God" in this classic passage is no different from the way "sons of God" is used with reference to angels in the story of Job.[72] "Sons of God" is certainly an appropriate way to describe angels, just as "sons of God" also describes those who are Spirit-led disciples of Jesus.[73]

It also has to be said that gods having sexual relations with humans, complete with human offspring, was standard fare in the mythology of ancient cultures. (One myth goes so far as to have the sons of God turning into oxen and siring donkeys, camels, and elephants!) So it would certainly be tempting to

---

71. Genesis 6:1-4
72. Job 1:6; 2:1; 38:7
73. Galatians 3:26; Romans 8:14

accept this interpretation of the account. For that matter, the notion of gods having human offspring is not altogether different from the virgin Mary being impregnated by the Holy Spirit and producing the Son of God.

There is also the fact that we angels can *eat* while on our earthly missions[74] (not to mention become objects of perverted lust, as in Sodom[75]), which might suggest to some that we could actually engage in sexual relations with humans, should we choose to do so. Certainly that was the interpretation drawn from the ancient Book of Enoch (to which Jude made passing reference in his epistle[76]), a story widely perpetuated to this day.

If I may say so, it's likely there never would have been any question about our procreating with humans had it not been for that enigmatic reference to "giants" — the ones who became the renowned heroes of old. "How else did those giants come about," rings the question from many, "except by some unauthorized angelic copulation with women?"

For those who insist on blaming the existence of giants on lustful angels, there is much to think about. Remember when the twelve spies were sent to scout out Canaan and ten of them brought back the discouraging report about the land being filled with giants? The fearful spies moaned about the Anakite giants they had seen — the descendants of Anak, who himself had descended from giants (namely Arba, the founder of ancient Hebron).[77] There were other "giants" encountered by

---

74. Genesis 18:1-8
75. Genesis 19:4-11
76. Jude 1:14
77. Numbers 13:25-33; Joshua 14:15

Israel during the period of the conquest, including the Emites (sometimes called Rephaites) who were just as tall as the Anakites.[78] (One of the Rephaites, King Og, had an iron bed thirteen feet long and six feet wide![79])

But don't forget the most important fact regarding any off-spring supposedly resulting from unholy liaisons between angels and humans. Without exception, each and every one of their original ancestors would have perished in the Great Flood, leaving no mixed angel-human bloodline to continue beyond that point. How then do you explain the appearance of giants *after* the Flood — including the Anakites, Rephaites, or even the notorious Goliath! The simple answer is that being a giant is a matter of *human* genetics, not the offspring of lustful angels gone wild.

So one would do well not to put stock in the "angel sex" rumor. Consider, instead, that the "sons of God" were the descendants of Seth and his son Enosh, who at first called on the name of the Lord but then went off the rails morally and spiritually, even marrying women who did not acknowledge God.[80] (Nothing to do, incidentally, with the relative beauty of the unrighteous "daughters of men" and the daughters of the "sons of God," as some have suggested.) If you wish to understand this intriguing passage, you must look at the context beginning in chapters four and five, where the wickedness of Cain's lineage is shown in sharp contrast to the godliness of Seth's lineage. It's on the heels of *that* discussion wherein you find this passage describing the devolving spirituality among even Seth's descendants, giving cause for universal destruction.

---

78. Deuteronomy 2:10-11; 2:20-21
79. Deuteronomy 3:11
80. Genesis 4:25-26

Even more crucially, as you can read for yourself, God was so upset with *mortal man* (his earth-bound creatures of *flesh*) that in his righteous anger he limited man's longevity to no more than 120 years.[81] As that penalty indicates, it was sinful *humankind*—not rogue angels—with whom God was upset. (To be sure, disobedient angels are, even now, bound for punishment. Peter talks about that punishment; Jude talks about it; and even Paul—all referring to the notorious uprising that took place in heaven, about which I can personally testify.[82] But that punishment has nothing to do with angels purportedly having sex with humans.)

There is this related problem as well. Since we angels do not die, is it to be believed that a contingent of wicked angels—living and cohabiting *as if human*—not only survived beyond the 120 allotted years, but *never* died? It can't be played both ways. If these were angels, they couldn't have been both human enough to have sex and unhuman enough never to die.

Apart from the sheer impossibility of sexual relations between spirit beings and humans, of greater importance is the fact that we angels neither marry nor reproduce, either in heaven or on earth. As you know, Jesus was crystal clear about that in his debate with the Sadducees regarding the Resurrection. As the Lord pointed out, along with not dying as man dies, the fact that angels don't marry is one of the most notable distinctions between angels and earthly mortals.[83] Marriage and procreation assume physical, genetic, biological, and emotional attributes that angels simply do not have—as will also be the case with resurrected humankind on the other side.

---

81. Genesis 6:3
82. 1 Corinthians 11:3-10; 2 Peter 2:4-10; Jude 1:5-7
83. Matthew 22:23-30; Mark 12:18-25; Luke 20:27-36

Not only was Jesus' point about the post-Resurrection paradigm lost on the Sadducees, but his mere mention of us angels drove them mad![84] Believing in no spiritual dimension other than this physical world, the Sadducees vehemently denied we even exist. In that, of course, they have common cause with the cynical materialists of your own day. As always with such sensual minds, it's only sex that ever matters. Sensualists cannot conceive of any dimension where sex plays absolutely no part. (And to think that, in a secular world, these are the renowned "intellectual Nephilim" of their time!)

Most important of all is what's so obvious from the passage itself. If you look closely you will see that these unholy marriages took place at a time when the Nephilim and men of renown *already existed*. Far from the Nephilim being the offspring of unholy liaisons, this much-debated passage states explicitly that when the sons of God had children by the daughters of men, the Nephilim were *on the earth* — and *also afterward*. Given the "before-and-after" time-frame specifically supplied by the text, I confess I'm mystified that the rumor about lustful angels ever got started!

Let's talk details...

*A*re angels ever female, or children? Ah, yes, I've heard the many expressions you use — like "she's an angel," spoken of a particularly lovely lady. Or "what a sweet little angel," inevitably said about winsome babes and darling infants. (Once again, of course, there's all that "angel art"

---

84. Acts 23:6-10

featuring golden-tressed women and chubby, rosy-cheeked babies to contend with. A picture is worth a thousand words...or misimpressions!) Even so, the short answer is no. Certainly no celestial angel has ever appeared either in heaven or on earth as an infant. And what you must understand first and foremost is that heaven is genderless — completely genderless, whether God himself or us angels. Whenever you see words like "Father" or "Son" attributed to God, the male gender is being attributed solely as appropriate to particular role designations. But because "spirit" is genderless, God, who is Spirit, has no gender. Nor do we.

It's a different story, of course, when we make earthly visitations. In our physical manifestations, nothing would prevent us from appearing in the feminine form. For whatever role God wishes us to play, whether human or otherwise, he gives us the power to "morph" into that role. But you would be right in thinking that in our *recorded* appearances we never appear as anything other than "men." (Don't be thrown off by those "two women with wind in their wings" whom Zechariah saw in the vision.[85] Had it not been for the mention of their "wings," it never would have occurred to anyone to think of them as angels.)

***H*ow many angels are there?** Only God knows. We spirits aren't into counting like you humans are. Whatever you do, don't waste your time with a calculator trying to add them all up! However tempting it is to take at face value some of the numbers appearing in the Scriptures, those figures aren't meant to convey mathematical precision. For one thing, you'd come up with completely different numbers,

---

85. Zechariah 5:9

depending on which text you happened to choose. Jesus himself spoke of "legions" of angels being available to him if necessary.[86] And, being present myself, I know that on Mount Sinai God surrounded himself with a host of angels as he delivered Israel's Law to Moses. Whereas some count that particular assembly in "tens of thousands," others more realistically speak in terms of "myriads."[87] And that's just the ones who made up the divine contingent on that spectacular occasion. Myriads upon myriads remained in the celestial realm, rejoicing from afar.

Surely by now you know that large numbers are symbolic of that which is either indefinite or innumerable. Does God have cattle "on a thousand hills"?[88] Yes, and all the other hills as well! On whatever countless hills they're found, all the cows are God's cows! And will God show his love to "a thousand generations of those who obey him"?[89] In this instance, "a thousand" is not to be taken literally, but means that God's love to those who obey him is endless. The same indefinite character attaches to Christ reigning "for a thousand years."[90] No literal "thousand years" is intended, but a sufficient time for God's purposes to prevail.

So when you read about "tens of thousands and thousands of thousands"; or "thousands upon thousands...ten thousand times ten thousand," you get the idea.[91] We're beyond counting, us angels![92] Best for you just to think of us as a whole *host* of angels![93] Stretch your imagination to the maximum, and then multiply that by...say, a *thousand*?

---

86. Matthew 26:53. (See Acts 7:53; Galatians 3:19; Hebrews 2:2)
87. Deuteronomy 33:2
88. Psalm 50:10
89. Exodus 20:6
90. Revelation 20:4-5
91. Psalm 68:17; Daniel 7:10; Revelation 5:11
92. Hebrews 12:22
93. 1 Kings 22:19; Psalm 103:20-21; Luke 2:13

Speaking of Angels

*H*ow many angels can dance on the head of a pin? You have no idea just how funny this question is to us angels, especially since we don't actually *dance* anywhere! Almost as much as you delight in thinking that we can "fly," we are downright envious that you can dance! Of course, I'm aware that this now-classic question has come to represent any conundrum to which there can be *no definitive answer*, but in truth there is a very simple answer to this particular question. It's all a matter of metaphysics, raising a question of importance not just regarding *our* nature but the nature of the *heavenly realm*. For if an infinite number of angels can fit on the head of a pin, then we have no material substance either individually or collectively. And if that's the case, then the heavenly realm is purely spiritual and matterless. On the other hand, if only some finite number of us could fit on the head of a pin (dancing or otherwise!), then the heavenly realm would not be altogether different in essence from the physical universe.

Since in fact the heavenly realm is purely spiritual and not composed of matter, then (despite our spiritual forms, or "bodies") in theory the entire celestial host of angels could easily congregate on the head of the tiniest pin, and we wouldn't even be crowded! But that's only part of the question, considering that we just as easily come and go between the heavenly and earthly realms. Whenever we're manifesting ourselves in *physical* form in the earthly realm, not even a single angel could dance on the head of a pin. (Can any human you know do that?) So obviously that's a whole different ball game. Then again, the fact that we are in physical form while on the earth doesn't mean that we are wholly and solely physical while appearing in human form. Though temporarily wearing a flesh-and-blood costume, as it were, we are still spirit beings operating on a spiritual dimension.

Angels, Demons, and the Devil

If I may be so bold as to say so, you are little different from us in that regard. Although you are presently unable to cross over into the heavenlies as we do, your earthly world has a spiritual dimension rarely appreciated on your side of the Great Divide. Like us, you too are a spirit being, yet temporarily clothed in flesh and blood. The time will come when your flesh-and-blood body will be transformed into a new, "perfect-for-heaven" body and fully share in the unencumbered spiritual reality of the heavenly realm. Indeed, one of the principal reasons we angels exist is to remind you of the intimate interface between the spiritual and the physical, the earthly and the heavenly. So—interesting as it is—never forget this classic question about how many of us can dance on the head of a pin. The implications for your own faith journey from the earthly into the celestial are rich with personal meaning. And that should set you dancin'!

*D*o angels have special powers? Yes and no. Compared with human capabilities, of course, we certainly have extraordinary power. Indeed, we are *mighty* powerful![94] (Think *dynamite*, since that's the root word.) But don't forget we are only messengers for God, so whatever power we exercise is really God's power. Perhaps you recall when David was being punished for numbering his troops (as if Israel's strength lay in sheer numbers rather than in God!).[95] Of the three options God gave David for his punishment, David chose for Israel to endure a three-day plague, described as "the sword of the Lord." But that "sword" (which destroyed 70,000 Israelites) was wielded by an angel of the Lord. That angel (whom David saw as if standing between heaven and earth) was set to destroy Jerusalem before God relented and stopped him.

---

94. Psalm 103:20-21; 2 Thessalonians 1:7
95. 2 Samuel 24:10-25; 1 Chronicles 21:7-30

But here's the important question: Was it *the angel* who destroyed the 70,000 Israelites, or *God* working through his angel? It goes without saying, really. The terrifying power of God's angel on this occasion was simply a manifestation of God's own power in the situation. The angel was merely God's personal conduit through whom punishment rained down on David and his people. (This was also true of the Lord's angel who put to death 185,000 men in the Assyrian camp, when Sennacherib's army got up the next morning and there were all those dead bodies![96])

The same goes for our role back in Egypt when God sent the plagues as a means of liberating his people from bondage. Whether it was the plague of flies, or frogs, or locusts, or hail, we were sent as God's destroyers.[97]

So are *we* powerful? No, but God is! Unless, of course, he chooses *not* to be, as was the case when Jacob wrestled all night with God.[98] (Because the prophet Hosea spoke of Jacob's divine wrestling partner as an "angel," we have some serious thinking to do a bit later....[99]) For his own reasons, God chose not to invoke the power in his hands that easily could have brought Jacob, not just to tears, but to the portals of death.

Which is good news for you! As with us angels, there is nothing that God's power in you cannot accomplish if that is his will. And more good news still is that God doesn't just destroy you in the snap of his finger, as he has the power to do! Which in turn is good news for us. We've never had to worry about using excessive power, even on those rare occasions when

---

96. 2 Kings 19:35-36
97. Psalm 78:49
98. Genesis 32:24-32
99. Hosea 12:4

we've been commissioned to bring about mass destruction. When God commands it, divine power is always under control and laced with divine integrity.

*J*ust how intelligent are angels? Oh very (he says modestly!). Billions of dollars have been wasted by earth's inhabitants searching for "intelligent life" out there somewhere. We celestials are not just intelligent, but possess a higher intelligence than our human counterparts. Yet to be fair, much of what passes for angelic intelligence is simply a greater awareness gifted to us by virtue of existing on a higher plane of reality—not to mention that we know pretty much everything about your own cosmos simply by observing it from the outside. Is that a higher *intelligence*, or merely a higher *perspective*?

Whatever it is, we clearly have a reputation that precedes us. For instance, don't you just love that classic encounter between the wise woman from Tekoa and King David?[100] Of course it was all Joab's scheme to convince David to bring his son Absalom back into royal favor. The wise woman's assigned role was to flatter David into softening his heart toward Absalom. And so she says to him things like, "My lord, you are like one of God's angels in discerning good and evil." And "My lord, you have wisdom like an angel—knowing everything that happens." You can almost see David's head swelling. What you humans say about flattery getting you anywhere certainly did the trick!

Well, I'm not sure how "wise" we are, but we do know pretty much everything that happens in the terrestrial realm.

---

100. 2 Samuel 14:1-24

Speaking of Angels

Sometimes more than we *want* to know! For example, Paul wasn't wrong when he said that the persecution of the apostles was a spectacle not only to men but also to angels.[101] Yes, we were watching...grimly. Orders we hoped might come to stop it never came. God has his reasons.

But you should not hastily assume that we are omniscient. Only God knows all. Like you, we know only what we're permitted to know. If we know far more than you at this point, that only speaks to relative knowledge, and often does not include the future. While we know some things about the future, we do not know all things. As I alluded earlier, we definitely don't know the day and hour when the earthly dimension will be brought to a glorious end, consummated in the Lord's return to judge the living and the dead.[102] We're all on stand-by alert for that Day!

In the meantime, we have been privileged to witness God's unfolding wisdom in the reconciliation not only between a holy God and sinful man, but between Jews and Gentiles in God's spiritual body on earth. What we've come to see is the stroke of divine genius in which Christ has become the common denominator for both forms of reconciliation. To our amazement, the incarnation into human flesh we could never have imagined being associated with God has enabled one barrier after another to be torn down. The art of divine reconciliation—once a mystery even to us—is now made clear to all![103]

In terms of spiritual matters, we're not mind readers. And we're certainly not infallible judges of the human heart. Indeed, the human experience is a phenomenon we have

---

101. 1 Corinthians 4:9
102. Matthew 24:36
103. Ephesians 3:7-13; Colossians 1:15-22

invested much interest in discussing among ourselves.[104] Not the least curiosity for us is how you can have the dual nature you have, being both physical and spiritual. Or how you can "die" yet "live eternally." Or how temptation works on you in the particular way that it does (so unlike our own temptations). Or how God worked out the whole plan of salvation before any of you ever sinned.[105] Or how God could be formed in a human womb and then die as you die. And, most of all (you may find this interesting), what it means to be pardoned for sin.

Oh, we certainly *rejoice* when a sinner turns to God! In fact, there's always a huge celebration with hosannas of praise to God.[106] Because we know human faith and repentance please God, we too are pleased! Who can't get caught up in the excitement? But don't forget that, for celestials, there is no "plan of salvation," as you would call it. No pardon for sin. And that has always intrigued us. "Does God love man more than angels?" we've wondered. (He certainly never transformed himself into one of us, as he has done for humankind.[107])

Yet we have come to understand that there is a very good reason why we are treated differently. Being in God's very presence not only eliminates any need for a trusting "faith" in his existence (how could you miss him!), but it also robs us of any excuse we might have to disobey what he commands of us. Greater is required of those to whom greater is given.

Not that humans have any excuse to sin (God even walked with Adam in the Garden!), but we appreciate that the gap between the human and the Eternal One is a yawning chasm compared

---

104. 1 Peter 1:12
105. Revelation 13:8
106. Luke 15:7, 10
107. Hebrews 2:14-18

with the celestial distance between the Eternal One and ourselves. If for no other reason than this, those among us who rebelled in the Great Uprising cannot claim injustice for their lack of pardon. Yet, we continue to be amazed at the loving and gracious character of a God whose most dominant trait (to us) is his complete and total sovereignty. From such an exalted Sovereign, could there possibly be pardon? What you may take for granted, we bend down to earth in wonder to behold!

Some bigger questions...

*a*re angels immortal? That all depends on how you define *immortal*. As I said earlier in passing, unlike you mortals who inevitably experience death, we angels never die. Which makes us immortal.[108] Yet some people have the mistaken idea that to be *immortal* is to be *eternal*, which would mean that, like God, we have always existed. That is certainly not the case with angels, otherwise we too would be God. We are celestial, but not divine; mere creatures, not the Creator.

Begging your indulgence, let me take a bit of a detour for a moment to set up a useful analogy. To speak of things "eternal" is to speak of *quality*, not *quantity*. Things that are "eternal" have an eternal *nature*, not an eternal *timetable*. For a human being to have "eternal life" is not to live forever and ever throughout endless years, but to have a life that (even on a time-bound earth) is infused with a measure of God's own eternal qualities. It is that same "eternal life" which ultimately finds its fulfillment in the timelessness of heaven.

---

108. Luke 20:34-36

In terms of salvation or condemnation, *eternal life* (after death) has its counterpart in *eternal death* (after death), which—at some point—will become the total and irreversible destruction of the soul. Focusing on a horrifying picture of agonizing torment day and night forever and ever obscures the awful finality of eternal punishment—that "second death" of which John wrote.[109] Think of it this way. Even in the midst of the worst possible agony, there is life. And where there is life there is hope. But for the wicked, in the end there will be neither life nor hope. Indeed, their hopelessness will be made all the more bitter by glimpsing the joys of the celestial realm, only to be thrown out into a state of permanent and darkened non-being.

It is this destructive "second death" which impacts the crucial issue of mortality or immortality. Man is mortal in the sense that all men die in the flesh—physically, biologically. But man—as a living soul which survives separation from the body at death—also has the potential for spiritual immortality. I say *potential*, because not every soul will enter into the eternal realm. Some will cause themselves to be cut off completely from their Maker, never to enjoy the immortality they were created to have. Remember when Jesus warned his disciples not to fear those who could kill the body, but rather to fear the One who could destroy body and soul in hell?[110] Although God created man for celestial immortality, with death being the divinely-designated portal from earth to heaven, God never assured immortality to every man.

Indeed, this was the intent of God's forewarning to Adam—that if he ate of the forbidden tree his *soul* would die. That he would forfeit life eternal. That he would not experience the immortality

---

109. Revelation 20:14-15; 21:8
110. Matthew 10:28

God desired him to have. Had God been speaking of physical death, Adam would have dropped dead the moment he took that first forbidden bite. Instead, it was his *soul* that died in that moment, as well as any chance Adam might have for immortality, without divine forgiveness from a gracious God. And since all have sinned, just as Adam did, all too have died spiritually.[111] Which is why, in love, God sent his Son so that whoever believes in him would not *perish*, but have eternal life; for it was not God's desire that any one of his creatures should suffer eternal death.[112]

With that detour behind us, let me turn back to our own angelic nature. As I said before, we angels are immortal, never dying as do humans. Even so, as spirit beings we share much in common with the spiritual souls of humans. Which is to say that nothing prevents our ultimate destruction in the same way that the souls of the wicked among mankind may be consciously punished as appropriate, but will ultimately be destroyed once and for all. I suspect you have many questions about the rebellious angels who even now are in quarantine; and about that "lake of fire" prepared for the Evil One and his co-conspirators. Suffice it to say with regards to angel immortality that nothing limits God from dispensing his judgment against wicked angels as he sees fit. Should he choose to impose conscious torment, that is his choice. Should he choose to destroy them completely, that is also his choice. Which of these two options (or indeed whether it might be a combination of the two) is a topic of hushed debate even here among us celestials. What is not in debate is that we are *immortal*, but not *indestructible*. For us celestials, it's a sobering thought. Is it for you as well...?

---

111. Romans 3:23; 5:12-14
112. John 3:14-16; 2 Peter 3:9

Angels, Demons, and the Devil

*D*o angels fear God? I can see why you might think so, and certainly those of us who are left after the Great Uprising cannot help but think about our destructibility. For it was the very lack of fear that led to the rebellion. In addition to a celestial hubris of the highest order, a kind of intimate familiarity had bred contempt among those who forgot that God was God and they were not. It still stuns me to think any angel could possibly be so bold! If anyone should know of God's unmatched power, presence, mind, and holiness, we angels should! Through overuse, you mortals have so eviscerated the word *awesome* that it's been robbed of all meaning. But in its purest sense, *awe* is really the only word to describe one's reaction to the sovereign God of heaven and earth!

So never fear, we faithful angels are always in fear! No, not in *cowering* fear, or *trembling* fear, or *frightened* fear, but *respectful* fear—fully aware that there is none like God.[113] I wonder, have the saints of God on earth become so familiar with God that they no longer fear him? If so, more's the pity. To lose a sense of overwhelming awe in the presence of the Eternal One should be your own greatest fear!

*H*ow and when did angels come into existence? As with humankind, the heavenly host of angels was brought into being by an act of divine creation. (We are included in the *invisible* part of all the things "visible and invisible" that were created.[114]) But unlike humanity, the sum total of celestial beings appeared simultaneously—neither multiplying by a process of procreation nor being added to in number at any subsequent point.

---

113. Psalm 89:5-8
114. John 1:3; Colossians 1:16-17

Incidentally, it would have been easy to continue that last phrase, saying "at any subsequent point *in time*." But we do not exist within a framework of time as you do. In the realm of the eternal, we do not think of "eternity" in the same way — as if "eternity" were an incalculable quantity of time. Or endless years. Or countless days. In truth, there is no such thing whatsoever as "time" on the other side. No hours, days, years, millennia, or eons. While you experience only a single lifetime (during which you might study the history of the world over the whole span of human existence), we angels have existed before all that ever happened, and will continue to exist long after the whole of human history has been written.

Yet that is not to say there are no points of beginning or ending within the eternal realm, particularly in relationship to time in the temporal realm of human observation. As we've already discussed, we celestials easily slip in and out of time. On each earthly mission, we move from the eternal to the temporal and back again. The playful phrase you sometimes use — going "back to the future" — is a natural and frequent occurrence for us. We think nothing of it!

So even though we are outside of earthly time, we can anticipate "the future" — such as the Lord's return to earth and the great Day of Resurrection in which we angels will be honored to play a part. We can also appreciate "the past" — such as when we angels were brought into being.

On the scale of eternity, therefore, we were created at a definitive point without that point actually being a point "in time"! If that's confusing, think about your dreams and how things might happen *sequentially*, yet outside of any time frame of which you are conscious. Only when you reawaken are you back in "real time" that never quite encompassed the events in your dream sequence. Clear as mud?

Relative to your own, earthly time frame, we celestials came into being before any earthly time frame ever existed. Which is to say, before the creation of your world. How long before? Any attempt to answer that would miss the whole point of the timelessness of heaven. All you really need to know is that when God announced his grand plan for creating mankind and then shared details of the marvelous cosmos he had designed for man's universe, the whole host of heaven listened in rapt silence. As he laid the foundation for this incredible new cosmos, we watched in unparalleled wonder and then erupted in spontaneous celebration! (The report of our jubilation in the story of Job hardly touches the hem of the garment in describing how excited we were![115])

With each day of Creation, we went crazy all over again. It was "good" indeed! We could hardly believe what we were seeing. If the physical cosmos pales in comparison to heaven's grandeur, it's only because heaven's grandeur itself is so sublime! Yet nothing God has created is without utter fascination for us. And when God capped off Creation with that first man and woman in the Garden, we were not just fascinated but delirious with excitement! Neither animal nor angel, a dual-natured humanity was a stroke of divine genius. And "*In God's own image?*" It was nothing short of stupendous! In stunned amazement, we shouted praise to God as never before.[116] If only you'd been there to hear the resounding chorus of adoration rolling like thunder throughout heaven! Short of the tumultuous reception we gave the risen Lord when he ascended back to the Throne after triumphing over death, there's never been a more joyous occasion in heaven!

---

115. Job 38:4-7
116. Nehemiah 9:6

Speaking of Angels

It's beyond anything you can relate to, but it's as if the whole of the newly-formed universe joined us in celebrating God's creation—from the farthest stars, to the highest mountains, to the creatures in the deepest depths of the sea. What a glorious hallelujah! Worthy of praise indeed is the Creator of All![117] The fact that large segments of humanity have come to debunk the whole process of divine creation is quite beyond us. If only they had witnessed what we ourselves saw, they would fall trembling to their knees! Indeed, one day they'll do just that.

I suppose we angels could have reacted with sibling rivalry at the thought of God creating other beings than ourselves. Apparently anticipating that possibility, God assured us that man would be created neither superior to ourselves, nor even equal, but inferior. "A little lower," I believe was the way God put it.[118] No offense intended. There are actually ways in which you have many advantages over us celestials, not the least of which is that God deigned to become like you in a way he never became like us. Just how amazing is it that the Eternal One himself should become "a little lower" than even we angels![119]

The other advantage you have is experiencing what you often speak of as "the best of both worlds." In heaven, we don't know the special joys of human love, or the rich intermingling of souls in marriage, or the special joy of having children and grandchildren. And never have we known what it's like to look up at the stars in the heavens with an unknowing wonder we celestials could never have.

Incidentally, you must never confuse "the heavens" with *heaven*. The created "heavens" encompass the entire physical

---

117. Nehemiah 9:5-6; Psalm 148:1-6
118. Psalm 8:3-5; Hebrews 2:6-7
119. Hebrews 2:5-9

cosmos, including earth, sky, sun, moon, and stars, and the vast universe of which you have but the slightest glimpse. *Heaven*, by contrast is the invisible, spiritual realm of the eternal. As wonderful as your universe is, the day is coming when the whole cosmic panoply will disappear with a roar, and the very elements of "heaven and earth" will be utterly and completely destroyed in a cataclysmic conflagration.[120]

Indeed, we can't wait to welcome you into our eternal home when the Lord returns to claim his own on that great Resurrection Day! Just don't be misled about the timing. Until the Resurrection at the Lord's coming, no soul will have entered into heaven. (Otherwise, what would be the point of the Resurrection? Or Judgment Day?) But I digress. As you already know, even the decaying Creation of which you are a part is (to personify an impersonal Creation) "groaning and longing" for the day when God's children by faith (even now spiritually *re-created*!) are fully revealed in resurrected glory.[121] Though we angels know what it means to be created, we can only speculate with wonder what it must be like to be created, then *re-created* spiritually, then resurrected to glory as co-heirs with Christ!

In and around heaven...

*A*re you suggesting there are no souls in heaven yet? I know you must get tired of my saying "yes and no" to so many of your questions, but I'm afraid that's exactly how it is in this case. Let me ask you this: What is there apart from the material world you live in except the spiritual realm of

---

120. Isaiah 24:3; 2 Peter 3:10-13
121. Romans 8:12-25

the eternal? You're right, nothing! So when the body is separated from the soul at the instant of death, does it not make sense that the soul can only be "in the eternal"? As between the temporal and the eternal, the dead certainly aren't "on earth," so they have to be "in heaven." In that limited sense, it was proper for Paul to speak of God's whole family "in heaven and on earth."[122] But that's where it gets complicated.

Think of it this way. Do you feel comfortable with the thought that Christians can be (and ought to be) "*in* the world but not *of* the world"? It's not exactly the same idea, but there is a sense in which a soul can be "in heaven" without actively *participating* in heaven. Without being *conscious* of heaven. If you promise not to think in terms of some "corner of heaven," I'll suggest to you that the realm of the dead (which I prefer to call *Sheol* since *hades* is too often confused with *hell*) is an intermediate state within heaven's eternity. Think of it as heaven's "waiting room," where the souls of the dead, both righteous and wicked, remain in repose awaiting the Resurrection and Judgment at the end of time on earth.

Do you recall the word most often used — even by Jesus — to describe death?[123] It's *sleep*, right? In Sheol, the souls of the dead are "sleeping," as it were, unconscious of their eternal state, and wholly unaware of what's going on around them in heaven (or, more certainly, on earth).[124] I realize this presents quite a different picture from the typical view conjured in Jesus' story of the rich man and Lazarus, where Lazarus is in Abraham's bosom having a conversation with the rich man in torment.[125] Yet, not only does that story have nothing to do with the Gehenna of *hell*

---

122. Ephesians 3:14-15
123. Mark 5:39; John 11:11-14
124. Job 3:13-17; 14:12; Ecclesiastes 9:4-10; Isaiah 26:19
125. Luke 16:19-31

(as *hades* is usually mistranslated), but Jesus was not intending the story even as a literal snapshot of Sheol. On the "other side," the righteous won't be discomforted by seeing their unsaved loved ones suffering in anguish; and certainly there are no *tongues*, parched or otherwise!

In this story, Jesus is meeting the Pharisees where they are in their own thinking about "Abraham's bosom" and "torment" and uses it as a teaching point to talk about the spiritual dangers of wealth ("the Pharisees loved money"), and about obedience to the Law and the Prophets which the Pharisees loudly lauded but blatantly disobeyed (as in divorcing their wives). Most importantly, Jesus uses the story to talk about there being no second chances after death.

When it comes to getting a handle on heaven, everyone's focusing on the wrong Lazarus. It's that *other* Lazarus — the one Jesus raised from the dead — who tells the tale.[126] Or, more importantly, *has nothing to tell*! Don't you just know that Lazarus would have been peppered with questions as he emerged groggily from the tomb? "What's heaven like?" "Did you see Abraham there?" And (undoubtedly) "What are the angels like?" But neither Lazarus nor any of the other people who were raised from the dead ever spoke a single word about heaven (or Sheol). I can also assure you that if they had ever had even a momentary glimpse of heaven, they would have been hugely disappointed finding themselves back on earth! (Heaven aside, old Samuel was upset even to be disturbed from his slumber in Sheol!)[127]

---

126. John 11:17-44
127. 1 Samuel 28:15

Speaking of Angels

As comforting as it may be for the bereaved to be told that their loved one is at this very moment with God in heaven (a divine judgment call, incidentally, which no man should presume to make!), the truth is that nobody gets to heaven before anybody else. That, of course, was the concern of the disciples in Thessalonica, who feared that, at Christ's coming their deceased loved ones might miss the boat. The apostle Paul reassured them that, on that Great Day when the Lord descends to claim his own, the dead in Christ will be raised (awakened!) and those who are still alive will be caught up with them into heaven's glory.[128]

Just as no one will be left behind, no one gets a head-start! Not even Enoch or Elijah, who were rapturously taken; nor Moses, who was transfigured on the mountain together with Elijah.[129] How all that worked is not unlike the way in which we angels appear and disappear. In fact, it was our "chariots" and "horsemen" who gave Elijah the ride of his life into heaven's "waiting room."

What even serious students of the Bible sometimes forget is that heaven and hell both await the coming Judgment, when the "sheep" and the "goats" will be parted right and left.[130] On that Day, the Lord will judge the living and the dead, the righteous and the wicked—all at once. Everyone must appear before the judgment seat of Christ so that each may receive his reward or punishment.[131] As you know, those are Paul's own words, no matter how much he desired to die "and be with the Lord."[132] It will be on *that day*, he said, when he and all the righteous will receive their crowns at the same time.[133]

---

128. 1 Thessalonians 4:13-18
129. Genesis 5:24; 2 Kings 2:11-12; Matthew 17:1-9
130. Matthew 25:31-46
131. Daniel 12:2, 13; John 5:28-29; 2 Corinthians 5:10
132. Philippians 1:22-24
133. 1 Corinthians 15:22-23; 1 Thessalonians 5:10; 2 Timothy 4:8

In reassuring the Thessalonians that those who caused them trouble will reap their reward, Paul was explicitly clear about when that will happen. It will happen, says Paul, when the Lord comes from heaven in blazing fire with all his angels. On the day he comes to be glorified, the wicked will be punished with destruction, while the righteous will marvel at God's glory.[134]

The divine sequence is crucial: No heaven or hell until Judgment. No Judgment until the Resurrection. No Resurrection until the Lord returns. And when he returns—trust me—no one living or dead will miss his appearance! The whole host of heaven will be there to make sure of that! My voice will be booming, I can assure you, and the entire cosmos will be trembling at its imminent destruction.

It was none other than the Lord who said that no one has ever gone into heaven except himself.[135] Nor did that change when Jesus told the thief on the cross that he would be in "paradise" with him that day, for not even Jesus ascended into *heaven* while his body lay in the tomb. (Remember his telling Mary Magdalene that he hadn't yet returned to the Father?[136]) As we angels can attest (for we were there on the occasion), Jesus did not enter back into heaven until his glorious ascension was witnessed by his apostles in the days following his resurrection.[137]

Jesus' conversation with the thief was about *salvation*, not *location*. About *spiritual identity*, not *geography*. As it happens, both Jesus and the thief *were* in the same realm of death at the end of that awful day of crucifixion—lying side by side, spirit to

---

134. 2 Thessalonians 1:6-10
135. John 3:13. See also Acts 2:29-35; Hebrews 9:28; 1 Peter 1:3-5
136. Luke 23:9-43; John 20:11-17
137. Acts 1:6-11

soul. But what's far more interesting is the way that story is even now being played out—as is the story of all humankind.

Remember our conversation about time and time-outside-of-time? And also what we said about death being a kind of "sleep"? Think, then, about what happens when you fall asleep. No matter how long you might sleep, the first thing you know after falling asleep is the moment you wake up. Right? That's how it will be when you die. No matter how much time transpires between your death and the Resurrection, it will seem to you as if no time at all!

Does it make sense, now, that heaven will dawn upon the thief as if it were opened to him the instant after he closed his eyes in death? Can you see how, even if Paul has to wait until Judgment Day to get his crown, nevertheless he could "die and be with the Lord" as if instantaneously? With such a felicitous ending all around, heaven can wait! In the meantime, don't forget the crucial sequence. First, it's the Lord's return. Only then follows the Resurrection and Judgment when the righteous shall awaken to discover their immortal resurrection bodies and the unrighteous are bound over to their just punishment and hell's destructive finality.

So is anybody in heaven yet? Not really...but just as good as!

So angels don't escort the souls of the dead to heaven? Or to Sheol! Seems like ever since we whisked Enoch away from earth—and Elijah, even more so—rumor's had it that we give every departing soul a personal escort to their final abode. That's how the popular tale Jesus repeated about Lazarus and the rich man came to include the bit about angels carrying the beggar to Abraham's bosom.[138] (Have you ever noticed, incidentally, that the rich man in the tale simply "died and was buried"? The Jews weren't ready to give *him* an angel escort!)

It's not as if souls need a "heavenly hearse" to transport their formless souls to heaven's "waiting room" in Sheol. (Do you need the help of angels to move from a state of being awake to a state of being asleep?) And since there's been no Judgment yet, as we talked about earlier, we certainly wouldn't be transporting souls directly either to heaven or to hell.

I'm aware that many people have something slightly different in mind when they think in terms of angels escorting the dead—that we, in fact, are the "grim reapers" sent to call souls home to God. That is not true, either. To begin with, there is no Grim Reaper, typically depicted as some ghastly figure in a black cape and hood, wielding a sickle to "harvest" the living when the time is ripe for their death. Besides which, God rarely chooses the time for each person to die. It is not his wish, for example, that innocent fetuses in the womb are put to death through abortion. Or that precious little ones die in childbirth— or that mothers themselves die in the process of giving birth.

To be sure, on occasion God has exacted the punishment of death, sometimes on a grand scale—first, in the Great Flood, and later in the deaths of men, women, and even children so as to wipe out the idolatry by which his chosen nation was repeatedly being seduced.[139] And certainly there have been times when we angels were specifically sent to "reap" a particular soul, as when one of our host was sent to execute a death warrant on King Herod for allowing himself to be worshiped as a

---

138. Luke 16:22
139. Genesis 6:5-8:22; Joshua 10:29-40; 1 Samuel 15:1-3

god.[140] But unless God has specific reasons for a particular death (and that's not always to do with punishment[141]), the fact is that death simply happens as a natural process, making possible the transition from mortality to immortality. In that process, time and chance play far more of a role than our knocking on your door saying it's time to go. It's like fish swimming into a net—some get caught, some get away to be caught another day.[142]

While death is said to be an "enemy" (because of the fear of the unknown that it evokes and because it brings such painful separation for those who are left behind), we on the other side view death in much the same celebratory way as you view a new life emerging from the womb. Despite the trauma associated with the "birth canal" of death, once the soul emerges on the other side, nothing of death's fear or pain remains.[143] Your *enemy* (and it is all of that!) is our *friend*.

That said, there is in fact a sense in which we will act as escorts for the dead—even as "grim reapers," sort of. That will come at the end of time when the Lord returns to bring judgment on all mankind. Ours will be the task of harvesting the "weeds," as Jesus referred to the wicked in his parable.[144] Which is to say that we will scour both earth and Sheol for every wicked soul who's ever lived, so that they might kneel before the throne of God's judgment to give account for their evil deeds and be sentenced to their eternal destiny.

---

140. Acts 12:19-23
141. Isaiah 57:1
142. Ecclesiastes 9:11-12; Luke 13:1-5
143. Isaiah 25:8; 1 Corinthians 15:25-26, 54-57
144. Matthew 13:36-43

That won't be a fun job, but we certainly will take great delight in our other task on that Great Day — gathering God's righteous elect from the four corners of the earth in a rapturous ascent to meet the Lord in the air. Everyone still living on that Day-of-Days will experience the Son of Man coming in power unlike anything they have ever witnessed, as if a trumpet were blasting throughout the whole cosmos.[145] Together with the saints in Sheol whom we will awaken to receive their eternal reward, the saints on earth will be transformed brilliantly into heaven's glory! Are you looking forward to that Great Day as much as we are?

*A*re the dead aware of activity among the living? Most certainly not! Solomon answered that question with an exclamation mark![146] I know there are those who would tell you that Moses and Elijah on the Mount of Transfiguration exhibited knowledge of earthy events, but I'm afraid they're reading into their Bibles what they want to believe.[147] That Jesus talked to Moses and Elijah about his forthcoming departure is a far cry from their already knowing about it on the other side.

When those same people urge that Samuel knew Saul was fighting the Philistines and already had a thorough knowledge of the whole situation, they betray their over-eagerness to believe their own imaginations. Saul certainly didn't assume Samuel had prior knowledge from beyond the grave, otherwise he wouldn't have felt the need to tell Samuel about the Philistines![148] Samuel's response did not reflect knowledge of

---

145. Matthew 24:30-31
146. Ecclesiastes 9:4-10
147. Luke 9:28-36
148. 1 Samuel 28:15-19

past events, but was a prophecy of the future—a prophecy which could only have come from God.

And you really know folks are grasping at straws when they suggest that the author of Hebrews had the knowing spirits of the faithful dead in mind when he wrote about that great cloud of witnesses surrounding those who believe.[149] Nothing of what he writes suggests that Abraham and Moses and David and all the others listed in "the roll call of the faithful" are literally looking from Sheol at the lives of living Christians. The Hebrew writer is figuratively picturing an amphitheater filled with the faithful, as it were, urging them on to victory. But it's a *picture*, not reality. Had the author wished to say that Abraham, Moses, and David were getting telepathic reports of your daily actions, I assure you he would have said so in no uncertain terms.

In the end, it is faulty eschatology that prompts such fuzzy thinking about what the souls of the dead know on the other side. If you get Sheol and heaven wrong, it all starts to unravel into unsubstantiated (and unworthy) speculation.

*W*hat more can you tell us about heaven? Everything and nothing. I'm permitted to speak to my heart's content about what heaven is like. It's just that not even I have the gift to communicate its truly stunning reality. (Remember when the apostle Paul got a sneak preview of heaven's glory in his mysterious vision? Not only did he hear things that no one is permitted to tell; more importantly, what he heard was *inexpressible*.[150]) Anything I could possibly

---

149. Hebrews 12:1
150. 2 Corinthians 12:1-6

say has already been said in visions and revelations using graphic word pictures and striking apocalyptic language to give you some *hint* of what heaven is like.

When Jesus said he was going away to prepare a place for his followers, he wasn't talking about some grand "mansion in the skies" you sometimes sing about.[151] I'm sure you already know that, but sometimes our attempts to explain the inexplicable do almost as much harm as good. Using material concepts always risks your thinking materially about something in a way which couldn't be farther from the truth.

The picture of heaven most people have in their minds — all those pearly gates and streets of gold — is more earthly than heavenly. Heaven has no gates, no streets, no gold! No mansions, no rivers, no trees! And I hate to be the bearer of bad news, but neither are there any pets in heaven, as many suppose. To think that there might be is to misunderstand altogether what heaven is about. It is a *spiritual realm* for *spiritual beings*."

Even when we speak plainly about heaven, there are many who disregard what hints we can provide. Consider, for example, when Jesus talked about coming again and taking you to the "rooms in his Father's house" which he had gone to prepare so that you yourself may be where he is.[152] It's not as if heaven were a "place," complete with postal code, to which you could be physically transported. And heaven is not really *up there* as you tend to think of *up* instead of *down* in a directional sense. *Beyond* might be a better word. Or perhaps "on the other side" might be helpful.

---

151. John 14:1-4
152. John 14:3

However you wish to think of it, you should not be confused about "the new heaven and new earth," as if "heaven" will be merely a rejuvenated planet Earth or an idyllic Eden restored. Oh, no! The "new heaven and new earth" which "came down out of heaven" in the vision given to John was a jasper-walled city, complete with a golden street, a crystal-clear river, and a tree bearing twelve crops of fruit.[153] But that vivid description was never meant as anything more than an apocalyptic image of a radically-different future construct—in heaven!—which will completely replace the present "heavens and earth" (meaning this present universe). Of this you can be certain: John's vision was not suggesting that the present heaven wherein we angels currently dwell will somehow be brought down into some kind of glorified Earth, or, worse yet, magically merged. Heaven forbid!

Where folks get into trouble on this is in missing the complex multi-layering of prophecy, at once referring to events soon to take place within the lifetime of the original audience, yet often having overtones for generations to come. The Revelation to John is chock-full of flashbacks to earlier scripture. The references to the "new heaven and new earth" cited by both John and Peter[154] are actually drawn from Isaiah 65, a careful reading of which will affirm that, in using that phrase, Isaiah was not at all talking about the eternal realm you associate with the word "heaven." Had he been, Isaiah would not have spoken of old men dying or children being born. Everybody, but everybody understands that in "heaven" where will be no death or dying! In truth, Isaiah was talking about the coming restoration of the nation, which would be a radically new

153. Revelation 21:1-5; 21:9-22:5
154. 2 Peter 3:13

paradigm compared with their then-beleaguered situation. So when Peter and John borrow that phrase by inspiration, they are simply pointing to a radically new paradigm *in* heaven, not *heaven come down to earth* in any conceivable sense.

If you insist on taking the "new heaven and new earth" literally you must also take literally John's reference to a thousand-year reign,[155] and to Christ's coming down from heaven *literally* on a white horse, with a sharp sword protruding from his mouth![156] Given what *we* know about the heavenly realm, these are mistakes that no angel would ever make.

The question which intrigues those of us on the Other Side is why anyone would even be tempted to hold such a reductionist view of the sublime realm with which we are so intimately familiar—as if for one moment we angels would prefer to be part of such a "more-like-earth-than-heaven" world. It occurs to us that there might be two primary reasons why humans would be attracted to such a misguided notion.

The first is simply that familiar earthly carnality always tends to blur that which is spiritual. You see this, for example, at the end of Jesus' ministry on earth. Despite Jesus' emphatic teaching about his Kingdom not being of this world.[157] Jesus' closest disciples were still envisioning an earthly kingdom in which they would rule politically.[158] Surely, so they thought, the "twelve thrones" Jesus promised them were meant to be taken literally![159]

---

155. Revelation 20:6
156. Revelation 19:11-15
157. John 18:36
158. Acts 1:6
159. Matthew 19:28

The second reason is truly troubling, which is the widely-held notion that God has unfinished business with the Jews. Listening closely to the conversation on earth about "end times" and "end things," what we hear from the halls of heaven is much talk about Jewish exceptionalism, and unfulfilled promises, and the need for a thousand-year earthly reign to fulfill those promises, or perhaps the need to fulfill the "forever" land promise God made to Abraham. (Nevermind that the word "forever" doesn't always mean *forever*.[160])

Even logically, the "forever" land promise is particularly problematic. How would the "land promise" work when the *land* in question is part of a planet and cosmos that will completely disappear at Christ's coming?[161] And isn't this a kind of (how do you say it?) "bait-and-switch" argument? You are first told that the land of Israel was promised to the Jews *forever*, and so presumably heaven (which everyone knows is *forever*) must necessarily be something associated with this present earth rather than some ethereal, spiritual realm. Gotta have *land*! But almost in the next breath you are assured that the "new earth" won't actually be the same as this present *physical* earth! So whatever happened to the *physical land* in this cosmic shell game?

The questions just keep coming. In this so-called "new earth," will the boundaries of the "forever" land approximate the current geographic boundaries of the Promised Land? And will that "land" be exclusively set aside for the Jews? Most important of all, what would be the *purpose* of that land? Will there be a temple in that land? Priests? Animal sacrifices?

Unfinished business with the Jews, you say? As loudly to us angels as to those standing at the foot of the cross, we heard the

---

160. 2 Chronicles 13:5; Joel 3:20; Psalm 49:11
161. 2 Peter 3:10

resounding cry that fell from the Lord's lips: "It is finished!" Underscored by the writer of Hebrews, the truth is that God has no unfinished business with the Jews. On the cross, Jesus died for the sins of the whole world, whether Jew or Gentile. "All Israel will be saved" beccause all the saved are spiritual Israel—the children of Abraham by faith in Christ Jesus.[162] Jews don't need *land*; they need a *Savior*. They don't need a *restored Davidic Kingdom*; they need the *Kingdom of heaven*. They don't need a *restored Temple*, but individually and collectively to *become temples* within whom God dwells. They don't need a *"new earth,"* but a *new heart* and a *new spirit*—just like everybody else on the face of the globe.

Even without having any explicit description of what awaited them at death, those ancient heroes of faith celebrated in the letter to the Hebrews were living their lives in expectation of "a better country—a *heavenly* one."[163] They knew they were but aliens and strangers on this earth.

I can personally assure you that the eternal home of the righteous is far superior to anything like the original Garden of Eden, wonderful as it was with its pristine rivers, trees, and fruits. Even using your most fertile imagination, you could not possibly conceive of the "new heaven and earth" paradigm destined to replace the "old heaven and earth" paradigm with which you are so familiar.

So don't think simply of a corrupt or fallen world being *renewed* to its original state (or even being "new and improved" like the latest soap-box detergent), but think of a totally different reality that is radically, transcendently, and mind-

---

162. Romans 11:25-32; Galatians 3:6-9
163. Hebrews 11:13-16

blowingly *different*! The "new heaven and new earth" will not be heaven *on earth* in any form whatsoever, but rather is *heaven itself*—the same ethereal, matterless, altogether-wondrous realm where we celestials now exist. Don't fall for imitations. Don't settle for anything less. If perhaps you're disappointed to hear that "heaven" won't literally be on a restored earth, or are disappointed that a more spiritual heaven doesn't meet your familiar, earthbound expectations, I guarantee you that heaven itself will not disappoint!

*a*re there harps in heaven, and singing? Want to throw in trumpets as well? The best answer, I suppose, is *sort of*! Despite the graphic description of harps and singing in John's visionary Apocalypse, surely by this time you must appreciate that the spiritual nature of heaven precludes literal harps and trumpets, and even singing—at least as you think of voices and singing.[164] As matterless spirits, we angels have no lips, lungs, mouths, or tongues with which to "sing" in the way you would envision. (Paul, of course, was speaking only euphemistically of celestial communication when he referred to the "tongues of angels."[165])

Even so, in heaven there is a celestial form of praise not unlike your own singing, except that it far surpasses even the beauty of human hymnody. Celestial song is as different from earthly song as human singing is from a dawn chorus of birds awakening you with their "singing" on a glorious spring morning. When you get to the other side, you'll see what I mean...and love it! Just as there is a "music of the spheres" in the cosmos,

---

164. Revelation 5:8-14
165. 1 Corinthians 13:1

in the celestial realm a sublime melody will linger on even after the music of the earth has long ended.[166]

But don't concentrate on the "singing" in heaven. Focus on the *praise*. Listen to what's being *said* when angels "sing." You could call our angel choir at Jesus' birth "singing" if you wish, but it didn't sound anything like "Joy to the World" — except for the words themselves, which conveyed very much the same meaning.[167] "Glory to God in the highest, and peace on earth." All glory to God, indeed! And (as in John's Revelation) "Worthy is the slain Lamb!" As long as you have tongue and voice to sing, sing those words! In heaven, we never stop proclaiming them — in our own "non-singing" but transcendent, artistic way.

Which is good news for those of you who can't carry a tune in a bucket on earth!

*C*are to comment on the so-called nine levels, or "choirs," of angels? Thank you for asking, actually. Not everyone knows what you're even asking about. For those who don't, I'll just say that it has nothing to do with robed angels singing in a church choir! It has to do with speculation about different ranks of angels. I fear that over the centuries many theologians have let their fertile imaginations run wild. Hierarchy is a divine concept that runs amok when carelessly handled by humans. The Medieval idea that because we angels are true spirit (and thus matterless) we must therefore be separate species, and must therefore also be ranked in a vast hierarchy from the topmost angel to the lowest is, well, ludicrous!

---

166. Psalm 19:1-3
167. Luke 2:13-14

Speaking of Angels

First of all, it defies the self-same human logic that gave it birth. How could any human being begin to understand, much less postulate some elaborate theory about anything that is matterless? And by what non-sequitur is it to be supposed that, simply by virtue of being matterless, each angel is a separate species, as if one were a fish and another a tree? Or that, even if we were that distinct, each and every angel would *necessarily* and *invariably* rank either higher or lower than other angels? I'm sorry, but what utter nonsense!

As with humankind, we angels are distinct in personality, in character, and in mind. We can freely choose to obey or disobey; to serve or not to serve; to praise or not to praise. And certainly we have distinct and differing gifts and responsibilities— whether with regard to thrones, dominions, principalities, or powers.[168] But the bold assertion that there is some kind of a hierarchical "Jacob's ladder" with the whole angelic host standing top to bottom on descending rungs of intelligence, knowledge, power, honor, or rank is human speculation gone mad!

After this rant, I suppose you'll want to ask me whether we angels ever have human-like feelings! As you can tell from my elevated tone, we are not devoid of emotion. If we can praise with utter joy, we can also despair at that which is not praiseworthy. Sadly, all this wild conjecture about angel hierarchy is far from praiseworthy.

Digging deeper...

---

168. 1 Corinthians 15:24; Colossians 1:16-17; Ephesians 1:21

*a*re there "elect" and "non-elect" angels? You're speaking, of course, of that line in Paul's letter to Timothy where he charges Timothy "in view of God and Christ Jesus and the elect angels," to keep the instructions given to him.[169] So, yes, there are elect angels. But that only begs the question of what you mean by "elect," or—more to the point—what Paul meant by using that term.

I started to say that the answer to your question is possibly blurred by what has become known as the "doctrine of election" over which there is much theological debate, as we angels are aware. But on second thought, it could be that the answer to your question might actually bring some clarity to that very debate. For surely you agree that however Paul used the term *elect* in speaking of angels is undoubtedly how he and Peter—even Jesus—used the term with regard to God's chosen people.[170]

Perhaps it would be helpful to begin the discussion by noting how the word *elect* is used when referring neither to angels nor to humans but to Christ himself. There is, for instance, Isaiah's prophecy of the coming Messiah where God says, "Here is my servant, my chosen one [or *elect*] in whom I find much delight."[171] There is also Peter's description of Christ as a "chosen [or *elect*] and precious cornerstone."[172] When Christ is the subject of the term *elect*, it's clear that his chosenness has nothing to do with any doctrine of "unconditional election" whereby souls are either lost or saved by sovereign decree. Which should put one on notice that use of the same term with reference to angels and humans was never intended to suggest any sovereign decree

---

169. 1 Timothy 5:21
170. Matthew 24:24, 31; Romans 8:33; Colossians 3:12; Titus 1:1;
     1 Peter 1:2
171. Isaiah 42:1
172. 1 Peter 2:6

declaring that *some* would be destined to obedience and glory while *others* would be destined to rebellion and destruction.

Put simply, whoever God's faithful servants are, they are his *elect*. For God has chosen them to duty, to service, to holiness, and to glory! We can discuss this further at another time if you wish, but let me just say that we angels were created with the free will to choose either obedience or disobedience to the Holy One whom we serve. Mind you, that's a genuine, un-fudged, unpredetermined choice — not simply choosing in ac-cordance with a "choice" previously made for us before we were created. A "choice" about which one has no real choice is no choice at all.

Unlike humans who have never seen God in his celestial realm, we angels have. You can appreciate, then, why angels are not called upon to "believe." We *all* believe! (For which reason even the rebel demons *believe*.[173]) Rather than being saved by faith (or lost for lack of it), we angels are called sim-ply to obedience, which — given our existence in the presence of God — should not be that onerous a demand. Yet, quite in-credibly, many among our angelic host did indeed disobey, re-belling against the God who had honored them with his very presence. That's another story for another time, but the point is that their disobedience was a free choice, willingly chosen. Had God somehow predetermined their rebellion, his fierce judgment against them would have made no sense. And let there be no doubt. Never have we witnessed such divine wrath either in heaven or on earth!

Of this one thing you can be certain: We angels who remained obedient to God were not pre-chosen or "elected" not to rebel.

---

173. James 2:19

And the angels who did rebel were not pre-chosen or "elected" to rebel. When the rebellion arose, each of us had a decision to make and we made it freely and voluntarily, unprompted by any behind-the-scenes orchestration, manipulation, or secret sovereign decree. We who are now in heaven are God's "elect angels" because we remain God's obedient servants—in duty, service, and holiness. Are you one of God's "elect" in that same sense?

Since even angels were able to sin, will we ourselves be capable of sinning in heaven? I see why you might feel disquieted by such a possibility, but the answer is unequivocally no. Nor will it simply be a matter of your no longer having free will. Having freely chosen in this life to be an obedient child of God, you will find that critical choice fully brought to fruition in the celestial realm. If it were nothing more than being liberated from your earthly body, at the very least you'd also be freed from your body's fleshly desires. Yet, beyond even that you will be wholly transformed in mind and essence so that nothing could possibly drive a wedge between you and God ever again. Not even the sins of the rebellious angels will be a temptation to you in your new state of being (nor to us!) At the Resurrection of earth's righteous ones, all will be made new! Complete and continuous holiness will be the eternal hallmark of God's faithful creatures, whether human or angelic. Praise be to the Holy One, the words *rebellion, disobedience,* and *sin* will never again have a place in the lexicon of heaven, for nothing impure will ever enter it.[17]

---

174. Revelation 21:27

Speaking of Angels

*D*o angels have a particular repugnance for slander? I suppose you could say so. Although no sin is greater than any other sin, it's no secret that the consequences of some sins are greater than others. And sometimes the very nature of a particular sin seems more abhorrent. In heaven, we've never known the same sins as you experience on earth. As I alluded earlier, we never had to struggle with sexual sins, or gluttony, or other sins connected to the flesh. The spiritual challenges we faced in the pre-rebellion era had more to do with thought and spirit. With attitudes and obedience. With truth and falsity.

Our "repugnance for slander," as you put it, undoubtedly stems from our experience with the Great Uprising. For when the Evil One and his angels initiated the insurrection, the recruiting tool found to be most useful (if you can possibly imagine it) was vicious slander against the Holy One! There is much more to be said later, but Satan actually had the temerity to malign God's very character, whispering among the host of heaven that God had ulterior motives for keeping us angels beneath him in an inferior and servile status. That God was simply on a divine ego trip at the expense of true love for his creatures. That he reveled in the potential for evil, as ultimately the existence of evil would serve to enhance his own sovereignty and glory.

Naturally, not a word of it was true. Why is it, do you suppose, that those who are bent on evil seem always to tar their opponents with the very evil with which they themselves are tarred? If there were any truth at all behind the slander, why not simply argue the righteousness of the cause itself without having to twist, distort, and deceive? Whether in heaven or on earth, slander is made necessary only because telling the absolute truth would reveal the slanderer's real motives and expose the weakness of his own position.

As you can appreciate, experiencing so unthinkable a celestial insurrection has had a lasting effect on the rest of us. Even now, it stands as a reminder of the evil of slander, whether against God, or other angels, or even the Evil One himself. And just in case you wonder, to characterize Satan as the "Evil One" is by no means slander. As unflattering as it may be, it is the absolute, unvarnished truth. No exaggeration, no embellishment, no twisting, no distortion. When the facts speak for themselves, there is no need for slander.

So it is that when the Evil One and I crossed swords over the burial of Moses' body, I did not slander Satan, but simply rebuked him in the name of God.[175] Under the circumstances, slander would have been superfluous. Nor, for the same reason, have we ever slandered any of Satan's co-conspirators before God. Resorting to slander would merely lower us to their same level.

That point seems to escape many on earth, including those who pride themselves in being God's specially-appointed guardians of truth. Never content to contend earnestly and honestly for the faith as they understand it, they seemingly can't resist bolstering their weak arguments with malicious slander of those with whom they disagree. Such arrogant men are so addicted to slander that no one is safe from their defamation. In the minds of false teachers, it's *everyone else* who gets labeled as a false teacher! I'm convinced that if they thought it would advance their own cause, they wouldn't fear slandering even us angels. They certainly wouldn't be the first to try![176]

---

175. Jude 1:8-10
176. 2 Peter 2:10-12; Jude 1:8-10

*I*n what way was the Law spoken through angels? I see you've been reading the letter to the Hebrews, which in itself is your first clue. When the gospel of Christ was first being preached, the Hebrews (or Christians of Jewish descent, if you will) were having difficulty coming to grips with a whole new faith paradigm. As you can appreciate, they assumed that the long-awaited Jewish Messiah would not alter in the least the Law, the prophets, temple worship, or anything else in their religious heritage. That would include their view of angels, which by the first century had developed into a rather exaggerated sense of our importance. Addressing this problem in his epistle, the writer makes a strong argument showing how Jesus — although made "a little lower" than the angels in his humanity — was, as the incarnate God, spiritually superior to angels.

Whereas God had spoken to Israel for centuries through the Law and the prophets, the letter to the Hebrews affirms that God has now spoken to the Jews (and Gentiles as well) through God's own Son, Jesus of Nazareth. That being true, the Son is superior even to angels, for it was through us that the Law had been given.[177] Not to confuse you, but there is a slight play on words involved. Although neither Moses nor the prophets were celestial angels, they were "angels" in the sense of being God's messengers to bring his revealed will to mankind. You may recall that, in his thoughtful response to Job, young Elihu spoke of "angels" or "messengers" through whom God has revealed himself to man.[178] But let's not detour too far from the role that we angelic beings actually played in the giving of the Law.

Do you remember the occasion on which Moses was given the Ten Commandments and the rest of the laws bearing his

---

177. Hebrews 1:1-4; 2:1-2
178. Job 33:23-28

name? You already know about the thunder and lightning, the sound of a trumpet, and the smoke coming from the mountain—all of which virtually scared the Israelites to death![179] What you've not been told directly is that a whole host of us formed God's entourage that day, embellishing his own awesome presence with our fiery chariots.[180] (Where there's smoke, there's fire!)

Our presence at the dispensing of the Law on Mount Sinai was not unlike our presence when the glory of the Lord appeared in Seir and Paran. On all three occasions, there were myriads of us holy ones in rapturous company with God.[181] When *he* appeared in glory, *we* appeared in glory!

By the first century, the Jews took great pride in telling anyone who'd listen how *their* Law had been sent from heaven by angels! All the while, of course, they were disobeying that very Law, and—as Stephen the martyr reminded them—had killed not only God's prophets, but the Christ himself whose gospel was superior to the Law we angels helped promulgate on Sinai.[182]

None less than the apostle Paul acknowledged our role when, in his letter to the Galatians, he said that the Law had been put into effect through angels. Mind you, the Law didn't *originate* with us. Although the Law came *through* us, it was *from* the mediating Messiah (even before he appeared in flesh, which once again suggests we still have much to talk about).[183]

---

179. Exodus 19:16-20:20
180. Psalm 68:17
181. Deuteronomy 33:2
182. Acts 7:37-38, 51-53
183. Galatians 3:19

One might possibly think that Paul was gratuitously throwing us into the mix when he warned the Galatians that any gospel contrary to that which he had taught them would bring eternal condemnation, whether that false teaching was from men or even from angels.[184] Of course, we angels don't preach *any* gospel of ourselves. We're only facilitators, as when we brokered Philip's preaching to the Ethiopian eunuch and Peter's preaching to Cornelius the Gentile centurion.[185] Given the danger posed by the persistent legalism of the Jewish believers in Galatia, Paul's reference to us was more than a subtle hint about the inferiority of the Law we angels had a hand in proclaiming on Sinai compared with the gospel proclaimed first by Christ and subsequently by Paul.

As important as the Law was in identifying sin and its consequences, it was never intended to bring justification by faith through Christ. If we angels must forever be associated with an inferior, transitional covenant between God and his people, so be it. We are happy to have played even that minor role. In the eternal unfolding of God's grand scheme for man's redemption, no role is ever really minor.

Let's get practical...

*D*o we have guardian angels? Well I've been waiting for this question. You'd have every right to think there are "guardian angels," wouldn't you? From what you've read of the angels watching over Lot, Isaac, Jacob,

---

184. Galatians 1:8
185. Acts 8:26-39; 10:1-48

Daniel and his three friends Shadrach, Meshach, and Abednego — not to mention Peter and John and Paul — there can be no doubt but that we angels have been assigned to guard a number of individuals throughout time.[186] But none of those instances really answer your question, do they? What you really want to know, I take it, is whether we are ever permanently assigned to each and every human soul as a kind of caretaker or patron angel protecting them from evil and harm's way. Am I right?

One could be excused for believing in guardian angels merely from reading about the incident where one of us facilitated Peter's miraculous jailbreak when he was imprisoned in Philippi. That single occurrence alone could certainly suggest the existence of guardian angels. And all the more so when the disciples who were praying for Peter's release were convinced (despite all their fervent prayer!) that they weren't seeing Peter himself at the front door, but only Peter's angel — as if Peter had a full-time angel assigned exclusively to him.[187] To make sense of their "angel comment," you have to understand that, by the first century, Jewish notions about angels were as fanciful as their notions about the Messiah. (Except for the Sadducees, who didn't believe in angels at all.[188])

You may also have read the psalmist's assurance of personal protection, saying that God will command his angels to guard you so that you can even tread on lions and cobras with complete safety, and that your foot won't crash against a stone.[189] If

---

186. Genesis 19:1-23; 48:15-16; Daniel 3:28; 6:19-23; Acts 5:17-20; 12:6-11; 27:22-24
187. Acts 12:1-17
188. Acts 23:6-11
189. Psalm 91:9-13

Speaking of Angels

I were you, I wouldn't test that theory in every detail! As ever, David and his fellow psalmists were much given to hyperbole when expressing the heights and depths of human emotion. I dare say even David the giant-killer would have thought twice about stepping on a cobra!

If it were true that everyone had a guardian angel, I'd need to have a serious talk with some of my celestial colleagues. Virtually all mortals have bumps and bruises, while others fall off mountains, jump from burning buildings, or die in the line of enemy fire. Were we the kind of Superman guardians everybody talks about, we'd have a pretty embarrassing track record.

Have you ever noticed how inconsistent most people are when it comes to talking about guardian angels? Say, for example, there's a car crash. Of those who survive, the talk is all about "their angels watching over them." But what about those who *died* in the accident? Were their guardian angels taking a coffee break at the moment of impact?

If you think in terms of evil, rather than physical harm, in what sense could we guard you against your own moral failings? In order to keep you from having lustful, or envious, or hateful thoughts, we'd have to get into the mind-control business. And if we *could* do that, but didn't, wouldn't your sin be as much our responsibility as yours? We're damned if we do, and damned if we don't! Did someone rob a jogger in the park? "Why didn't the robber's guardian angel step in and stop him?" one is entitled to ask. "And why didn't the jogger's guardian angel prevent the heist?" To take the words of the psalm literally is to miss the point.

Even the Evil One wanted to make capital out of that comforting psalm when he quoted it to Jesus in the wilderness of temptation.[190] But Jesus wasn't about to fall for such nonsense. To be sure, legions of us would have rushed to Jesus' rescue had he fallen from a high pinnacle of the temple, but Jesus would never have put that proposition to the test, and neither should you.

What Jesus knew (and what you can take equal confidence in) is that whatever adverse circumstances come your way, there is comfort in knowing that all adversity can be endured through faith in a God who cares what happens to you. In the further-ance of his kingdom, God may indeed call upon us to protect you from some specific harm, physical or spiritual. Or perhaps open and close doors to guide you in a certain direction so that his eternal plan might be accomplished. But that's a far cry from each of you having your own celestial bodyguard.

Much has been made, of course, of Jesus' mention of angels in connection with children, suggesting to many that each child has a guardian angel.[191] You must be careful, however, not to skip over the context. Jesus wasn't suggesting that everyone comes into the world with his or her own personal protector — else what are we to make of all the children who die in the womb, or at childbirth, or perhaps sometime later through some awful tragedy, hunger, or disease. Again, what kind of guardians would we be to let all that happen (not to mention the utterly repulsive cases of child abuse)?

Check again and you'll find that Jesus' comment did not focus on the *children*, but on those who would mislead, tempt, and abuse them. When we angels see innocent children being led astray by callous, wicked people, we immediately look toward

---

190. Matthew 4:6
191. Matthew 18:5-14

God to see when and in what way he wants us to bring his judgment to bear on these unspeakable creeps! (Angels actually line up to volunteer for that duty!) But *guardian angels* for all children...and the adults they eventually become? Simply not true. (Not even *one* angel, much less the *two* assigned to each person by the teaching of Islam.)

So what do angels actually do for us? Behind the scenes, we are ministering servants working on God's behalf to bring his kingdom to full fruition. It is on *your behalf* that we serve—and for all who will inherit eternal salvation.[192] As God's agents in heaven and on earth, we're not in the business of making guest appearances. We're in the kingdom-advancing business, not the "touching" business. If people are "touched by an angel," it's only because something in that touching will further the interests of God's kingdom or the salvation of his people.

You can see a long history of our ministering to God's people— all with the unfolding eternal plan as the object of the exercise. Think, for example, of the time one of us accompanied Abraham's servant on his mission to find a suitable wife for Isaac.[193] God was intimately involved in every detail of the lineage through which one day he himself would be born into the world.

You can see that same emphasis on lineage in the widely-known dream Jacob had of the ladder (or staircase) on which angels were ascending and descending.[194] Even though it was only a dream, God used the imagery of angels to convey to

---

192. Hebrews 1:14
193. Genesis 24:7, 40
194. Genesis 28:10-17

Jacob the mystery of Christ's incarnation (seen in the descending angels) and his resurrection and ascension back into heaven (seen in the ascending angels). And with that picture came the good-news promise that through Jacob's descendants would come the hope of salvation for the whole world — a promise fulfilled in Jesus of Nazareth, a descendant of Jacob. Like bookends, first promising and then confirming the fulfillment of the promise, the imagery of Jacob's ladder and the angels reappears in Jesus' remarkable conversation with Nathaniel. But this time the "ladder" is the Son of Man himself, and Nathaniel is to be an eye-witness of the ascension Jacob had seen only in a dream.[195]

Yet it was not simply a prophecy of far-distant events that God brought to Jacob. In that same dream, God promised Jacob that he would watch over him until he brought him back into the land of promise. "I will not abandon you," God assured him. That's where we angels came in, being assigned to watch over Jacob throughout his travels. At a place he later named Mahanaim, we met Jacob to reassure him of God's continuing presence.[196] We ministered to Jacob right up to the time when he wrestled with the Lord — a special divine presence we need to talk about momentarily. As a prime progenitor of the nation which later would bear his name, Jacob (Israel) was a special object of our ministry to God's people. Not all of God's people get the same attention, but when God has some special role or gift or blessing in mind for you, we're there to bring it to you.

In the past, that has even included providing meal service! The most dramatic instance was when we were put in charge of delivering each morning's manna for the Israelites, and later

---

195. John 1:50-51
196. Genesis 32:1-2

the meat that fell out of the sky in the form of flying birds.[197] We weren't just serving "angel food" as if it were some humanitarian airlift to keep the Israelites from starving. It was God's way of moving his story along to the point where his Son would eventually be the Bread of Life feeding all of mankind spiritually.[198]

There was also the time when God's prophet Elijah fell exhausted beneath the broom tree, understandably depressed after fleeing from that wicked woman, Jezebel. One of us was dispatched to deliver a "take out" meal of fresh-baked bread and a jar of water.[199] Elijah couldn't believe what he saw...or tasted!

Perhaps no greater comfort can come for believers than knowing just how committed God is to protecting his own when they are on missions for the Lord. Consider, for instance, the time when the city of Dothan was surrounded by the Arameans in their pursuit of the prophet Elisha. Elisha's servant was ever so alarmed when he looked out and saw the hills filled with horses and chariots. But Elisha quickly calmed him by having his eyes opened to see an army of us angels ready to come to their defense.[200] Elisha's words to his servant have been a source of assurance for believers ever since: "Those who are with them are no match for those who are with us!" Whatever forces might come against you, they are never a match for the Lord's forces.

Nor can I forget the time when we were called into service to minister to the apostle Paul as his ship was tossing violently in

---

197. Psalm 78:18-29
198. John 6:25-59
199. 1 Kings 19:5-8
200. 2 Kings 6:13-18

the Mediterranean. The angel on duty that day brought words of assurance and comfort to Paul, telling him that he would be saved from the storm along with all who were sailing with him.[201] God didn't call us into action simply because he was feeling sorry for his anxious apostle. He was ministering to Paul so that Paul, in turn, could continue to minister to generations yet unborn through letters he would write while a prisoner of Rome.

No angelic missions were ever more meaningful to us, of course, than the times we ministered to the Lord himself, especially on the two occasions of trial when he needed us most. First, there was the forty-day period in the desert when the Evil One was doing his best to thwart Jesus at the very outset of his earthly ministry. Not only did Jesus need physical strength to endure his long fast, but during that time he was also vulnerable to ferocious animals which could have torn him apart. Our job was to see that didn't happen.[202]

And then in those excruciating final hours in the Garden of Gethsemane on the night in which the Lord was betrayed, one of the cherubim angels stood by him like a silent sentinel of strength — whose celestial familiarity reminded Jesus of his true home on the other side and the purpose for which he had become embodied as a human.[203] While not even the presence of the angel fully allayed Jesus' human apprehension and agony, it reassured him of his Father's love, allowing Jesus to bend his will fully to his Father's plan for man's salvation.

It was in those two periods of temptation that we angels came to appreciate most fully the mystery (even to us!) of the

---

201. Acts 27:23
202. Matthew 4:11; Mark 1:12-13
203. 1 Timothy 3:16

incarnation of the divine into the human. Never in all eternity could we believe God would actually lower himself to be *fully* human and to truly be tempted as man is tempted, or to experience what it's like to face death. To say that we ministered to Jesus on those occasions is hardly the complete story. (How could we angels possibly provide strength to the Eternal One!) Indeed, it was he who ministered to *us* in that ultimate act of humility, sacrifice, and love. It is *we* who came away all the stronger for having witnessed his finest hour![204]

Are we, then, ministering servants sent to serve those who will inherit salvation? Absolutely. Just don't think of us as fixers or fairy godmothers, or constant companions fending off every enemy or temptation. In furtherance of God's kingdom and your salvation, ministering to your long-term spiritual needs is never quite the same as fulfilling your immediate wishes.

Nor must you forget the now-greater role of the Holy Spirit working directly in the lives of God's people. Those who in faith have been baptized into Christ have the gift of the Holy Spirit in a way the ancients never did[205] — producing abundant spiritual fruit for the building up of Christ's spiritual body on earth.[206] Who even among the ancients of faith was ever blessed to have the Spirit helping them in their weakness, interceding in their prayers with groans that human words cannot adequately express?[207] How very blessed you are to have not simply the aid of angels — which the ancients experienced — but the soul-penetrating Holy Spirit living within you![208]

---

204. 1 Timothy 3:16
205. Acts 2:38; 5:32
206. Galatians 5:22-23
207. Romans 8:26-27
208. 1 Corinthians 6:19

Angels, Demons, and the Devil

*D*o righteous angels ever cause us to sin? Are you kidding? You must be referring to the vision given to Micaiah in response to the four-hundred false prophets who lied to King Ahab about the upcoming battle being a piece of cake.[209] What Micaiah saw, of course, was a vision in which the Lord assembled a counsel of his angels to ask how Ahab might be enticed to his death. When one of the angels suggested putting a lying spirit into the mouths of Ahab's prophets, the Eternal One approved the plan and sent the angel to do just that.

If that sounds like an open-and-shut case of celestial sin-mongering, I'm here to tell you that no such celestial counsel or conversation ever actually took place (anymore than Israel's literally being scattered like sheep on the hills, a scene which Micaiah also "saw"). Much the same as Nathan concocting a hypothetical story to rebuke David for his adultery,[210] and Jesus telling the parable of the murderous tenants to point an accusing finger at the Pharisees,[211] Micaiah's vision was simply a clever means of letting Ahab know that his prophets were lying to him. The vision was meant as wry irony, and it did the trick! The response to Micaiah from Zedekiah the prophet was dripping with even greater sarcasm. Yet in the end it was Micaiah's prophecy that proved true.

Trust me on this one. If you lie, or cheat, or get drunk, or envy your neighbor, don't blame it on us! And on the flip side of the coin, neither could we possibly separate you from God's love, even if we wanted to. God's love for you is constant and unyielding.[212] It is only you yourself who can throw away your

---

209. 1 Kings 22:7-28; 2 Chronicles 18:6-27
210. 2 Samuel 12:1-12
211. Matthew 21:33-46; Mark 12:1-12; Luke 20:9-18
212. Romans 8:35-39

inheritance by turning your back on God. It wasn't God who stopped loving the Evil One, but the Evil One who stopped loving God. So don't go there!

Wrapping it up...

*I*s there anything more you can say about angelic assemblies? Not much, really, other than that their importance is generally overstated. Apart from Micaiah's tongue-in-cheek story told for Ahab's benefit, there's really very little to fuel all the speculation among your scholars about our celestial confabs and conversations. Of course, there are the angels who present themselves before the Lord in the story of Job, but that discussion is better left until later. Perhaps you're wondering about Psalm 82 which speaks of God presiding in the "great assembly," giving judgment among the "gods."[213] I appreciate how one might conclude that these "gods" must be angels, since we're often referred to as the "sons of God." But if you take a close look at the psalm, I think you'll see that Asaph is referring to an assembly of human judges into whose presence comes the God of Justice himself. The obvious message is that Israel's judges must no longer be guilty of injustice against the vulnerable and oppressed while rendering decisions on God's behalf.

Because of the systematic miscarriage of justice in Israel, the judges were subject to God's wrath coming down on them in the form of death. What's more, in their deaths they would be no different from ordinary men or rulers, despite the fact that they thought of themselves as virtually self-appointed "gods."

---

213. Psalm 82:1-8

(If you've ever encountered some of your federal judges, you may be familiar with this particular hubris!) Naturally, the prospect of a death penalty couldn't possibly apply to us angels since, being spirits, we're not subject to death as you are.

If you have any lingering doubts about the meaning of this passage, you may wish to re-visit the words of Jesus when he quoted from Psalm 82, speaking — not of us angels — but of Israel's judges to whom the word of God had come in the form of a sharp stick.[214]

*W*hat is meant by the term *angel of God*? Let me ask you a question. Would you find it remarkable if someone spoke of, say, "prophets of God" or "children of God"? No? Because we angels all belong to God, in a similar fashion we too are all "angels of God." Or, "angels of the Lord." It's that simple. We "angels of the Lord" are featured everywhere in Scripture, going about God's business — whether accompanying Jacob on his journey, rebuking Israel at Bokim, giving directions to Elijah, wiping out 185,000 Assyrians, or pulling off jail breaks for the apostles.[215] There was also that line from the apostle Paul to the disciples in Galatia, saying they had welcomed him as if he were an "angel of God."[216] So that's it, really.

Well, actually it's not quite *that* simple. In fact, it can get downright complicated. You'll probably recall my hinting several times that we had much to talk about later. The time for

---

214. John 10:22-39
215. Genesis 32:1-2; Judges 2:1-5; 2 Kings 1:3, 15; 19:35; Isaiah 37:36; Acts 5:18-20
216. Galatians 4:14

that discussion has come, but first let me begin by laying a foundation of sorts. There's been a good deal of conjecture even among us celestials as to why God chose to create angels and work through us. Many of us have come to wonder whether it wasn't a matter of some necessity given the vast disparity between God and humans.

If only you could experience God in his full glory as we do, you'd instantly understand. As a mere mortal, you would be totally overwhelmed — in fact virtually *obliterated* — by the full power and majesty of God. Therefore, he tempers his divine presence for your benefit. In order for God to interact with mankind without destroying you in the process, either he must himself become fully incarnate (as happened in Jesus of Nazareth) or he must make use of other intermediaries such as ourselves. Sometimes, as I've explained, we manifest ourselves as normal human beings, attracting no particular attention to ourselves as angels. But whenever we have appeared in our more celestial state, we have exhibited something of the supernal brilliance of God's majesty, yet without literally blinding those to whom we have appeared. Make sense so far?

Now think of those times in Scripture when seeing an "angel of God" was extraordinary even by normal angel standards. From what they saw, witnesses didn't just talk about angels, but concluded they'd seen the face of God! Lucky for them, that's not exactly true since God's untempered presence would consume them. Which explains why God didn't allow Moses to see his "face," but only his "back" as he passed by. In the words of God himself, nobody who sees the face of God could live to tell about it![217]

---

217. Exodus 33:12-23

In that regard, don't be misled by the occasion on which Moses, Aaron, Nadab and Abihu, and Israel's seventy elders dined with God and "saw him" without the least harm coming to them.[218] What they saw was a rather splendid representation depicting God's presence, right down to the translucent pavement of sapphire under his feet. A compelling image, to be sure, but not truly God. (It was just visual enough to assure them that God was "at table" with them, without being anything more tangible that they would have been tempted to reproduce by way of an idol.)

So what was it people saw when they encountered the "angel of God" or "angel of the Lord"? When he wasn't appearing in human-like form, God sometimes associated himself with fire and flames. In those instances, you'd do well to think in terms of God's aura, or personna, or alter ego. The word *penumbra* also comes to mind—a word which describes the light emanating along the outer edges of a darker surface, as when the moon is in an eclipse. In whatever way you might describe the phenomenon, the "angel of the Lord" on those rare and special occasions was not a member of our angelic host, but a personal manifestation of God himself—the "angel of his presence"![219] (Ever wondered how God could have *walked* with Adam and Eve in the Garden?)

Perhaps no better example exists than what Moses experienced at the burning bush.[220] "The angel of the Lord" appeared to Moses in flames of fire within the bush; but, as you know, that "angel of the Lord" turned out to be none other than God. Understandably, Moses was scared to death to look at God—

---

218. Exodus 24:9-11
219. Isaiah 63:9
220. Exodus 3:1-6; Acts 7:30-32

or, in this case, even God's flaming aura. So when you read in your Bible about the "angel of the Lord," you have to ask yourself whether it's a normal angel or a divine manifestation of God himself (a *theophany*, as theologians like to speak of it).

Even before appearing to Moses, God had appeared to Jacob both in dreams and "in person," in the form of the man with whom Jacob wrestled. After each event, Jacob realized he had been visited by the Sovereign God. In one dream, the "angel of God" specifically identified himself as "the God of Bethel."[221] And in the latter instance, Jacob said he had seen God "face to face."[222] No wonder, then, that Jacob (renamed Israel) later referred to God as "the Angel" who had delivered him from all harm.[223]

Another good example is when "the angel of the Lord" appeared to Gideon in Ophrah.[224] No burning bush this time. No flames. God appeared as a normal human being (just as we angels often do), whom Gideon assumed was a holy man of God. When "the holy man" caused fire to consume some meat and bread on a rock, then suddenly disappeared, Gideon realized to his horror that he'd been talking "face-to-face" with the Sovereign God of the universe! He was so discombobulated that God had to reassure him he wouldn't die.

Something similar happened when "the angel of the Lord" appeared to Samson's parents to tell them of his coming birth.[225] Manoah's wife assumed the strange visitor was a man of God

---

221. Genesis 31:10-13
222. Genesis 28:10-17; 31:10-13; 32:24-32; 35:5-10; Hosea 12:2-5
223. Genesis 48:15-16
224. Judges 6:11-24
225. Judges 13:1-23

and even wondered if he might be an angel because of his awesomeness. In the end, she was stunned to conclude that she had seen the face of God! It certainly wasn't one of us, I assure you. What all three of these incidents have in common is that God became his own messenger, which is to say *angel*. Purely in terms of physical appearance, what these people saw was not *an* angel (belonging to God) but *the* angel of God (his very presence).

We angels take great delight in one of God's more interesting personal appearances—to the hapless Balaam and his talking donkey.[226] You know the story. Because he sees "the angel of the Lord" standing in his way, the donkey goes where Balaam doesn't want him to go, or doesn't go at all—for which he is repeatedly beaten. Resentful, the donkey starts complaining to Balaam, who seems to take it in stride, as if talking to donkeys is something that happens every day! Finally, Balaam's eyes are opened so as to see "the angel of the Lord" for himself, and he gets the message. As Balaam goes on his way, he knows he has encountered, not just some run-of-the-mill angel of the Lord, but the Lord's very own countenance.

When God appeared to Hagar as "the angel of the Lord," there was something extraordinary about his presence that told her exactly who he was. "I've seen the One who sees me!" she said jubilantly.[227] Yet, the next time she encountered "the angel of the Lord" she didn't *see* him but *heard* him, speaking to her from out of heaven.[228] (In case you're wondering, God doesn't always use his booming voice, as when he spoke to Jesus, and the crowds thought it was either thunder or one of us angels

---

226. Numbers 22:21-35
227. Genesis 16:7-14
228. Genesis 21:15-19

shouting![229] Sometimes he uses his "still small voice" library whisper.) Following so closely on the heels of their first encounter, Hagar had no doubt about who was talking to her.

Hagar was not the only one to hear "the angel of the Lord" calling out from heaven. Just as Abraham was about to thrust the knife into the body of his son Isaac in the sacrifice God had instructed him to make, God's voice suddenly sounded (*booming* this time, I assure you), telling Abraham to stop. I must say we angels were holding our collective breaths until we heard God's voice stopping that knife! (On occasion, incidentally, "the angel of God" not only *spoke* from heaven, but could be *seen* in the "heavens above." That stunning "cloud by day" and brilliant "pillar of fire by night" leading Israel out of Egypt was in actuality a manifestation of the Lord himself.[230])

If you wonder about the ease with which God communicated with Abraham there on the mountain, don't forget all the previous times God had spoken with the ancient patriarch—and particularly the time when God showed up at Abraham's doorstep with those other two "men." It's almost as if God was wanting to highlight the similarities and differences between us angels and "the angel of the Lord." Just as we did that day, God took on human form and even ate with Abraham.[231] But as the Lord dispatched the two angels to Sodom to protect Lot and destroy the cities of Sodom and Gomorrah, Abraham quickly realized that the third "man" was neither man nor angel, but (as he referred to him) "the Judge of all the earth."[232]

---

229. John 12:28-29
230. Exodus 13:21-22; 14:19-20
231. Genesis 18:1-15
232. Genesis 18:16-19:3

Proceeding to bargain with God in an attempt to prevent the destruction of those wicked cities, Abraham knew he was being incredibly audacious by daring to address the Lord in that manner. And that goes double for us. If you want to know where angels fear to tread, *that's* where—bargaining with God! We're still amazed at how God puts up with things in man that he'd never tolerate in us angels.

Do you find all of this as fascinating as we angels do? But it gets even better. To say that "the angel of the Lord" is often *God himself* is not always the final word. Let me take you back to when God told Moses that he was sending an angel ahead of the Israelites to lead them into the land of promise.[233] If perhaps you've ever been tempted to think that God was speaking of me, his dutiful archangel (since protecting Israel was one of my major responsibilities), have you possibly overlooked a couple of important details? Remember when God said that his angel would not *forgive* the Israelites if they rebelled against him? As merely an angel and not God, I have no power to forgive anyone. Besides, they wouldn't have been rebelling against *me* but against God!

More significant still is God's saying, "my Name is in him" — as if to say his own Divine Self would be in this "angel." Again, that wouldn't be me. And since those two niggling details rule out *any* angelic beings as the "angel" to whom God was referring, who does that leave...?

Take a closer look at the time just following this when God reiterates his promise about the angel who is to lead Israel in driving out the Canaanites, Amorites, Hittites, and all the rest of the people inhabiting the land God was giving Israel.[234] This

233. Exodus 23:20-23
234. Exodus 32:33-33:3

time, God is angry at the Israelites for worshiping the golden calf, so he says something which might seem really odd. Having renewed his earlier promise about the "angel" being with them, God says firmly, "But I'll not go with you, because I just might decide to destroy you!" (And he wasn't kidding.) Yet then he turns right around and says to Moses: "My Presence will go with you"![235] Are you confused? How could God both *be* with them and *not be* with them?

As you can appreciate, the fullness of the divine godhead is not a great mystery to us. But we celestials can certainly understand how it could be a great mystery to you. God's unique complexity is sublime indeed, and — in terms of human understanding — virtually inexplicable. Even so, you must find the clues you've been given ever so tantalizing. Consider, for example, that mysterious reference to God's *Name* being in this "angel." Think about it. Who was given the name *Immanuel*, meaning "God with us" (as if to say, in him My Presence is with you)?[236] And who other than God the Father has the power to forgive sins?[237] It can be none other than Christ, the Son of God. Or to put it in words you might find strange: Jesus *before* he was Jesus! The Incarnate God *before* he was incarnate. The Son of Man *before* he took on mortal flesh and blood.

If ever you were curious, does this not explain Jesus' enigmatic reference to Abraham's having seen him?[238] When else would Abraham have *seen* the Lord except when he came into contact with the preexistent, pre-incarnate Logos — that "angel of the Lord" so evident throughout Israel's long history?

---

235. Exodus 33:14
236. Isaiah 7:14
237. Matthew 9:5-6; Mark 2:1-12; Luke 5:17-25
238. John 8:56-58

Am I seeing some disquiet in your face? Do you find this difficult to believe? Paul may have been using multiple layers of
prefiguration in his classic passage about Christ, but don't
minimize the truth of what he told the disciples in Corinth:
"Israel drank from the spiritual rock that accompanied them,
and that rock was Christ."[239] As strange as it might seem to
you, the pre-incarnate Christ literally traveled with Israel,
nourishing them spiritually along the way. And protecting
them as well.

Do you recall when Joshua was near Jericho and encountered
the man bearing the drawn sword? To Joshua's amazement,
the man introduced himself as "commander of the army of the
Lord" and accepted Joshua's instinctive reverence, as only the
Divine One could do.[240] What's more—just as with Moses
standing before the burning bush—Joshua was told to remove
his sandals, because he was standing on holy ground. Who
could that "commander" have been but the Lord Christ!

This should get you thinking again about what aspect of God's
multi-faceted persona appeared to Moses in the burning bush.
And what about that fourth "man" that King Nebuchadnezzar
saw in the fiery furnace along with Shadrach, Meshach, and
Abednego—whom the King described as looking like "a son
of the gods"? Since you and I know there is no plurality of
"gods" but only the One God, Nebuchadnezzar was more correct than he ever could have imagined. The one he saw was indeed the Son of God!

It was the same Son of God who, through the Spirit, preached
righteousness to Noah's contemporaries who died in the

---

239. 1 Corinthians 10:1-5
240. Joshua 5:13-15

Flood, "even those who are now dead" and whose disobedient spirits are awaiting Judgment in Sheol.[241] The same Son of God who, through the Spirit, preached the gospel of righteousness to the Israelites in the desert as he was leading them.[242] And the same Spirit of Christ working through the prophets of old, ironically predicting his own forthcoming earthly ministry and suffering![243]

One especially insightful prophetic appearance came in the form of a night vision to Zechariah, in which Zechariah sees various angels talking with "the angel of the Lord" who is standing in a grove of myrtle trees. Later in his series of visions, Zechariah sees the Evil One standing in the presence of "the angel of the Lord," being rebuked for opposing Joshua the high priest.[244] Who else would that have been but the Lord Christ? Even in visions, the prefiguration of Christ comes ringing through!

If I may say so, the way God has revealed himself to mankind from the beginning until now is truly extraordinary. How Christ could be active in the world before he was incarnate, then fully appear in the person of Jesus of Nazareth, then reappear resplendently both in Paul's Damascus Road vision and in John's apocalyptic revelation fairly boggles the mind, whether human or angelic![245]

Ever want an angel in your life? Naturally we're flattered, but how about having "the angel of the Lord" in your life! Undoubtedly you've read what David said in his psalms about

---

241. 1 Peter 3:18-4:6
242. Hebrews 4:1-6
243. 1 Peter 1:10-12
244. Zechariah 1:1-17; 3:1-10
245. Acts 9:3-6, 17, 27; 22:6-9; Revelation 1:12-16

"the angel of the Lord" driving away one's enemies and en-
camping around those who fear him to bring deliverance.[246]
Now that you know "the angel of the Lord" is often none
other than God himself—even in the person of the Lord
Christ—are you not highly comforted knowing it's more than
just one of us ordinary angels who is your greatest Protector?

*W*hat role will angels play in the final Judgment?
First and foremost, we'll be there to lend dignity,
honor, and majesty to that eminently solemn occasion. When Christ appears from heaven to judge the resurrected
souls of all mortals, we will provide the celestial backdrop to his
Throne of Judgment, watching in rapt attention as he divides
the "sheep" from the "goats," the righteous from the wicked.[247]
(When Jesus said that *we* would be the ones to separate the
wicked from the righteous and throw the wicked into hell, he
was not suggesting that eternal life or death would be our call—
only that we would be his agents of punishment.[248]) Those who
have confessed Christ before men, Christ in turn will acknowledge before us, while those who have refused to confess him before men will be disowned before us.[249]

Judgment Day will be a doubly sober occasion for us since we
are already painfully aware of the eternal destruction awaiting
our former colleagues. And to think that you mortals will be either acknowledged or disowned right there in the presence of
the entire angelic host![250] Not to put any pressure on you, but
have you ever considered that, at the Judgment, your holiness

---

246. Psalm 34:7; 35:5-6
247. Matthew 25:31-46
248. Matthew 13:49-50
249. Luke 12:8-9
250. Matthew 16:27; Mark 8:38; Luke 9:26; 12:8-9; Revelation 3:5

cannot help but be compared with ours? If God charges his angels with sin, how much more humankind made of dust![251]

Then again, have you considered that your holiness will in turn judge both the rebellious angels and the unrighteous among mortals?[252] Their spiritual insurrection against God cannot help but be compared to your own faithfulness, just as Noah "condemned" his generation by his faith.[253] Which is all the more reason to take your holiness and faithfulness seriously. Whether men or angels, none of us can escape inevitable comparison. It's always either *judge* or *be judged*!

*H*ow are we to understand the many angel references in Revelation? First of all, consider the nature of the writing itself. Like much of the figurative language in Isaiah, Ezekiel, and Daniel, the Revelation given to John on the island of Patmos is apocalyptic in nature. Which is to say that it is prophecy couched in the language of metaphor, pictures, and graphic imagery of a type that might be associated with a dream...or even a nightmare! In part, at least, it's a colorful caricature of a reality that can't otherwise be easily explained. (Or, for good reason is obscured just enough to confuse anyone who would use it for their own perverted purposes.) So don't focus on the imagery itself as if you could discover arcane meaning in each and every detail. That's not the point. Instead, follow the story-line, which you can best understand by knowing both the historical context and the audience to whom John is writing.

As you know, the first part of the Revelation is fairly straightforward — well, at least as straightforward as a revelation from

---

251. Job 4:17-21
252. 1 Corinthians 6:1-3
253. Hebrews 11:7

the ascended Christ can be![254] Those opening "letters" to the seven churches of Asia are like a State of the Union speech in which things are in a pretty sorry state. The message from Jesus to his disciples in those struggling congregations is that they need to get their spiritual act together. To persevere in their faith. To endure in the face of temptation. And to overcome whatever trials come their way. Why all these warnings? Jesus wants them to know that the persecution they experience will sorely test the limits of their faith. Lukewarm faith won't do. Nominal Christianity will leave them vulnerable. Anything less than total commitment will spell disaster.

As with all prophecy, John's vision contains multiple, overlapping layers of application—some of which pertain to John's immediate audience and some to generations yet unborn. (Wasn't that true of all the Old Testament prophecies?) Even the dual reference to "what is now" and "what is yet to come" bears this out.[255] And in a quite mysterious way (even for us angels), the warning of a coming time of persecution and judgment is as applicable to you as it was to John's first readers— as is also the repetitive theme-line calling these saints of God to sexual purity, honesty, and faithfulness in a culture of rampant idolatry.[256] (Who are the 144,000 that everyone loves to talk about? Those who remain faithful and morally pure.[257])

Yet, beyond the warnings comes a more important message— a prophecy of encouragement for a people under spiritual siege. It is a powerful, larger-than-life message of hope, victory, and ultimate triumph. To him who overcomes will be

---

254. Revelation 1:1-2
255. Revelation 1:19
256. Revelation 21:6-8
257. Revelation 14:1-5

given a new name![258] To him who overcomes, honor and authority will be given![259] To him who overcomes will come the privilege of sitting with Christ on his throne![260] At the climax of God's eternal plan, faithful saints and courageous martyrs have nothing to fear from "the second death." They will reign with Christ in glory![261]

Once you know the story-line, the role played by the angels in John's vision must surely become clear. By this time, what is the one thing you know about our work? As seen in the history of Israel, when are we most likely to appear? Is it not when God's judgment is imminent? And when is God's judgment imminent? You've got it. Both *now* and *later*. *Now* before you die, for after death it's too late for you to overcome. And *later*, at the Last Judgment of all mankind, which with each passing day looms nearer and nearer. Little wonder we angels are all over the pages of Revelation! Announcing the warnings. Announcing the promises. Announcing the judgments. Announcing the victories. Announcing the beginning and the end; the end and the beginning![262]

The fearsome yet hopeful picture Jesus depicts for John is painted on a broad panoramic canvas. So don't go crazy with the details. As for the mysterious cast of characters in the Apocalypse (especially us angels), don't try to read too much into who we are or how we operate from a narrative never intended as anything other than a story. A *true* story, to be sure,

---

258. Revelation 2:17
259. Revelation 2:26
260. Revelation 3:21
261. Revelation 2:11
262. Revelation 4:6-8; 5:8-14; 6:1-17; 7:1-3, 11-12; 8:2-13; 9:1-16; 10:1-11; 11:15; 14:6-20; 15:1-8; 16:1-21; 17:1-18; 18:1-3, 21-24; 19:4, 9-18; 20:1-3; 21:9-17; 22:1-7, 16

but one told *as a story*. Concentrate too much on the "trees," and you'll miss the "forest." Look too intently for meaning, and you'll miss the message. Read into the details what was never there in the first place, and you'll end up reading a completely different story. See it only through earthly eyes, and the heavenly will escape you. See it only through futuristic eyes, and crucial lessons for today will be wholly lost.

If you'd like a summary of John's Revelation from an angel's perspective, it all boils down to this: Keep yourself pure and faithful until death, and God will take care of the rest. Praise the Lord, he's already taken care of it!

Part Two

Speaking
of the Devil

To reign is worth ambition, though in Hell:
Better to reign in Hell than serve in Heaven.

— John Milton, Paradise Lost

Now that we've discussed angels, I know you're anxious to
hear about the one angel who, over time, has gotten by far and
away the most press. Isn't that the way it is? It's the bad guys
who stir up the most interest and grab the headlines! Not that
I'm envious in the least. I much prefer the shadows to the limelight. The problem with the limelight is that it exposes one's
flaws all the more clearly. Indeed, it can *create* flaws, as with the
Evil One himself. He had so much of the celestial limelight that
it went to his head. But I'm sure we will get to all of that soon
enough. So tell me, where would you like to start?

Angels, Demons, and the Devil

Is **the devil real?** Absolutely! If anyone should know, it would be me. In the period of celestial peace, we all shared sweet fellowship together among the heavenly host. When that peace was shattered in the Great Uprising, I suddenly found myself having to wage face-to-face battle against the Evil One and his supporters. Even now I warily monitor his every move. Would that he were only a figment of an overactive imagination, or merely a metaphor for evil, but I assure you he is more real than real! Really deceptive, really contemptuous, and really evil.

And what a waste. The Evil One was not always evil. He was once regarded as the Enlightened One, the one whose glory and resplendence was unparalleled among all the angels. Yet that very resplendence became his undoing, with disastrous consequences even for humankind. In fact, had it not been for his pride getting out of control and twisting him into a pitiful creature not even he himself can love, no evil ever would have besmirched heaven's holiness. Nor, likely, would evil have entered that pristine Garden below.

Just imagine it: Had the Resplendent One not become the Evil One, conceivably there might never have been any sin whatsoever. Wishful thinking, I know, and water under the bridge. But I can't help thinking what might have been.

What **happened in the Great Uprising?** At first, it seemed like nothing, really. A word here, a glance there. Everything easily could have been explained as wholly innocent. But as these things go, whether in heaven or on earth, there is a kind of creeping incrementalism that eventually transforms itself into what, looking back, one can see was a hidden agenda all along. Seems that the Evil One, as I now call him, had aspirations to be like the Holy One himself. No, to be *greater* than the Holy One, were that possible! It was not enough to be honored with special splendor and responsibility, or to be adored among the angels. Indeed, all that attention seemed only to feed his pride and swell his ego. Some of the angels even sought him out for advice and direction rather than approach the Throne. Not that the Holy One had ever given any reason whatsoever for resentment or disloyalty. Just the opposite.

It wasn't long before cliques were forming among the hosts of heaven. Then camps. Then armies! There was growing talk of mutiny and rebellion, and all of heaven was astir. I myself confronted the Evil One over his instigation of the Rebellion, but the warmth we once shared had turned to an icy reception as if we were immortal enemies. His terse, cynical explanation was that the Holy One was acting selfishly in not sharing his full glory. Can you imagine such an indictment against the very One who had brought him into existence and showered him with incomparable glory!

Quite incredibly, he also charged the Holy One with being unloving. And why? Because the Holy One dared to make a distinction between himself and his servants! For reasons I will never understand, the Evil One was particularly piqued that, despite his resplendence and special powers, he would always remain but a humble servant at God's throne. "Hierarchy! Hierarchy!" he kept shouting angrily, as if any structure or relationship involving headship or authority were inherently offensive. I wondered to myself whether he objected even to the Father being head over the Son.[263] Nor did it escape me that my role as archangel must have been a deep-seated cause for irritation. What I saw as a call to greater responsibility, he saw only as offensive "Hierarchy!"

---

263. 1 Corinthians 11:3

Angels, Demons, and the Devil

In truth, I suspect that the Evil One's sanctimonious railing against hierarchy betrayed his own insertion of power into the notion of hierarchy. Even among humans, there are those who project their own flawed character onto others, assuming that everyone else must surely act with equally questionable motives as themselves.

Looking deeper, it's clear why the Evil One was so offended. His problem was not really with the idea of *hierarchy* as power, for *power itself* was the very thing he coveted! Nor could he have been genuinely upset about simply the notion of hierarchy, since, as leader of the rebels, he certainly had no qualms about being at the top of the pecking order! What really irked the Evil One was that, for the moment, he had neither the power nor the vaunted position he so desperately wanted— namely, God's! As it would turn out, power and hierarchy would become hallmarks of this hypocritical "ruler of the air." (Do you find it as interesting as I do that political and religious critics who object most to hierarchy and power are the very ones who end up being the most intolerant and controlling?)

Over and over again, the Evil One kept returning to his bitter theme, seemingly oblivious to how humbly the Sovereign Lord of the Universe served his loyal retinue as much as we served him. Heaven was always—how do you say it—a "win-win" situation? There was no cause for discontent. Yet there it was in the very halls of heaven—envy, jealousy, resentment, and rebellion—all spawned by consuming pride.

The more we talked, the more heated and pointed came the slander issuing forth from the Evil One. More true of him than any since: None is more convinced of the rightness of his cause than someone who is so clearly wrong. Mystified and dumbfounded, I left my twisted colleague to his mad delusions.

Speaking of the Devil

At the time, I was unaware of the scheme already devised among the rebels to recruit to their perverted cause the newly-created man and woman in the Garden. It was a brilliant strategy. In one fell swoop the rebels could swell their ranks with a race of humans that would be ever multiplying (something angels cannot do), and — more sinister yet — would rob the Holy One of the unabashed pleasure he took in creating this new human race in his own image.

Maybe I'm more skeptical than is warranted, but in hindsight I strongly suspect that the Evil One personally saw the seduction of humankind as a means of achieving his coveted role as Supreme Ruler over all creation, both celestial and terrestrial. I also suspect that he was more than a little perturbed at the thought that "man" had such a special place in God's heart. Call it the sibling rivalry of a petulant two-year-old.

Whatever the motives, the stage was set for an all-out assault on two fronts. You will already be familiar with the successful seduction of the first couple. Nor would the Evil One be disappointed that, generation after generation, the offspring of these two progenitors would fall for all the same seductive lies, just as he calculated. With perverted pride, the Evil One would indeed become known as the ruler of their world (your world), though in no sense would he ever replace the Holy One's absolute sovereignty. Petulant two-year-olds can easily live in a fantasy world with complete contentment.

Not even God's summary judgment in the Garden seemed to unnerve the Evil One. Why should he care that the serpent was brought down to the dust? As with the man and the woman, all these lesser creatures were merely utilitarian objects suitable to his own selfish purpose. Nor in his arrogant stupor did he give any credence whatsoever to the Holy One's warning: "He will crush your head."[264] The Evil One was too buoyed by his easy victory there in the Garden and by the heady thought that his imminent overthrow of the Holy One would be equally as easy.

Upon the Evil One's return from his bold assault in the Garden, the battle in the celestial realm was fully joined. Yet despite the ferocity of the conflict, the outcome was never in doubt. It's not as if the Evil One and his rebels could actually have dethroned the Holy One. But that didn't lessen either the fierceness of the battle or the crucial deployment of divine power necessary to reach the foregone conclusion. The same would be true of every spiritual battle ever fought, either now long past or certainly in the future. When John's Apocalypse reprises this "war in heaven" in the context of first century persecution, it underscores the certainty of the Holy One's ultimate victory, no matter what the relevant circumstances might be.[265]

Incidentally, you should not think of this celestial battle in terms of your own wars, where men fall to their deaths. Angels don't experience death as humans do, not even on the field of conflict. So the number of the heavenly host that rebelled against the Holy One was the same number that survived the battle, only to be punished for their mutiny. (Be careful not to assume that precisely "a third" of the heavenly host was involved in the Great Uprising, as some have taken an oblique reference in John's Revelation to suggest.[266] That figure is not to be taken literally any more than the notion that precisely "a third" of the earth was burned up at the sound of the first trumpet, or precisely "a third" of the sun, moon, and

---

264. Genesis 3:15
265. Revelation 12:7-9
266. Revelation 12:3-4

stars was intended at the fourth trumpet.[267] What I can assure you is that the number of angels caught up in the Rebellion was beyond all earthly appreciation.)

How did God punish the insurrectionists? When the battle finally ebbed and the outcome was certain, angels on both sides of the divide stood in rapt attention wondering just what the Holy One would do with the rebels. It wasn't what any of us had expected. Unlike the holy wrath he displayed during the battle, the Holy One's countenance now betrayed neither resentment nor bitterness. There would have to be punishment commensurate with the offense, of course, but the Holy One was not about to lower himself to the level of those who had challenged his sovereignty. There would be justice, not retaliation. For the moment, he would do no more than what was needed to ensure heaven's purity and holiness.

Consistent with that aim, the sentence was banishment to "the other side" — where the Evil One had transformed a pristine, good world into a corrupted world of evil by introducing sin to humankind. Where else could the Evil One and his angels abide? Certainly not in heaven!

Yet their punishment would not turn out to be quite that simple. As hinted at in John's Apocalypse, the rebels faced a more torturous and final destruction.[268] Of that they were solemnly assured. In the meantime, they were to be relegated to exile in the Abyss of Tartarus for a period not unlike the "thousand years" of John's Revelation (which, given its apocalyptic genre, is neither literal nor precisely chronological).[269] Because

---

267. Revelation 8:7, 12
268. Revelation 20:10
269. 2 Peter 2:4; Jude 1:6; Revelation 20:1-3

time to angels means nothing, everyone knew it signaled a period of isolation prohibiting any further harmful interaction with humankind. Nor would their exile be a pleasant experience. In human terms, the Abyss would be like a fiery furnace, yet darkened from thick smoke.[270] In angel terms, it was the height (or indeed depth) of humiliation.

And never more so than for the Evil One. There in that squalid dungeon, the Evil One would finally become what he had so longed to be: a king. King of the Abyss! But instead of his being honored as, say, the Glorious One, or the Eternal One, or His Magnificent Highness, the names given to him—Abaddon and Apollyon (meaning Destroyer)—would forever mock his faux kingship.[271] If indeed the Evil One was finally Ruler over all he surveyed, what he surveyed was greatly to be pitied.

What can one say but "How the mighty are fallen!"[272] Suddenly, along with the Son himself, I too witnessed the Evil One fall from heaven like a lightning bolt![273] It was the most fearsome celestial occurrence I have ever witnessed, or ever hope to witness.

For Satan and his rebel angels, the story would not end in the Abyss. A time would come (during the earthly ministry of the Son and his chosen apostles) when they would be released from exile "for a short while" and thereafter be recalled to the Abyss to await the Great Day of final judgment and their ultimate fate in the "fiery lake."[274] In his prophetic depiction of that final judgment, Isaiah sees the Lord completely devastating the earth,

---

270. Revelation 9:2
271. Revelation 9:11
272. 2 Samuel 1:19, 25, 27
273. Luke 10:18
274. Jude 1:6; Revelation 20:3, 10

after which "the powers in the heavens above" are herded to-gether with earthly kings and bound in a dungeon.[275] By the time of that cataclysmic conclusion, of course, the former power and celestial presence of the Evil One and his angels will be but a distant, fading memory.

More about all that later. But the time-line I've just now given you will become absolutely crucial to our further discussion. Already before you ask me all the questions I anticipate, I know that some of my answers will assume periods of time in which the Evil One and his angels are confined to the Abyss, while other answers will assume these evil creatures are on the loose and doing some heavy damage.

Even when Satan's not personally running around on a short leash, the damage done by the Evil One from the very begin-ning is so pervasive that, like someone "speaking from the grave," Satan's power remains painfully manifest even when he is confined. Or to change the metaphor, while Satan is in the Abyss he's like an imprisoned Mafia boss still very much in control of the mob despite being behind bars.

Before we move on I should probably say just a word about the well-traveled notion that Satan's fall occurred long prior to the creation of the earth and the temptation in the Garden. That scenario is certainly a tempting idea, perhaps avoiding a number of difficulties. But it runs headlong into its own set of problems, the chief obstacle being the stubborn fact that had the physical universe not already been in existence, there would have been no "other side" for the Evil One and his an-gels to "fall into." To be "cast down to earth" requires the presence of an earth onto which one can be cast down!

---

275. Isaiah 24:1-3, 21-22

In truth, the Abyss of Tartarus (not to be confused with the *Gehenna* hell of final punishment) is not exactly on planet earth, as might be suggested from the phrase "cast down to earth." Nor is it some burning cauldron beneath the surface of the earth as one might surmise when Paul talks about every knee bowing at the name of Jesus—whether in heaven, or on earth, or *under* the earth.[276] (Though that imagery isn't far off the mark.) Think of it this way: If heaven were the left-hand page in a book and earth the right-hand page, the Abyss of Tartarus would be hidden in the crack between the two pages. What's important is not geography, but ignominy. As far from heaven as east is from west, the Abyss is a suitably ignominious realm for its shamefully ignominious inhabitants.

*D*oes the Great Uprising explain Paul's enigmatic reference to the angels? I take it you're referring to the phrase "because of the angels" in Paul's first Corinthian letter?[277] If so, the answer is yes, though it's not without complexity. As you know, Paul was addressing the controversy in Corinth regarding head-coverings for women.[278] In a careful balancing act, Paul affirms both the creational equality of male and female (neither is independent of the other) and the hierarchical relationship between the two (as Christ is the head of man, man is the head of woman).

Prompted by Paul's earlier statement that, in Christ, there is no distinction between male or female,[279] it seems that some of the women in Corinth had removed their traditional veils as a

---

276. Philippians 2:10
277. 1 Corinthians 11:10
278. 1 Corinthians 11:3-16
279. Galatians 3:28

statement of perceived emancipation. Pointing to the quintessential example of headship between equals (God being the head of Christ), Paul insists that equality in Christ does not preclude male spiritual leadership. Rather than generally imposing head-coverings on women as a sign of the woman's submission, Paul explains why their removing the customary veils in this instance was making a wrong statement.

Your question arises when Paul further marshals the rationale for maintaining hierarchical distinctions. "For this reason," says Paul, *"and because of the angels,* the woman is to have an authority symbol covering her head." Here, the apostle is referencing the Great Uprising in which the Evil One and his angels rebelled against the hierarchy of heaven. At first whispered, then voiced openly, their primary complaint was having to submit to the Holy One's divine authority — as if by that submission they were somehow second-class citizens. In their heady quest for liberation, they failed to appreciate the crucial difference between spiritual leadership and what they considered to be raw power-mongering. It's a mistake many have made, including, most notably, those who have been given the responsibility of spiritual headship.

Paul is not the only writer to refer to the Great Uprising. Jude does as well, describing how the rebel angels were dissatisfied with their rank and station in heaven and consequently fell from their natural realm.[280] To lose sight of where the Holy One has called each of us to be has been the downfall of many, both in heaven and on earth.

---

280. Jude 1:6

*C*ould Satan have kept from sinning? What are you suggesting — that somehow God *needed* Satan to sin in order for his sovereign plan to unfold? Or that God himself orchestrated the Great Uprising for his own purposes? You can forget that! Whatever God might presciently know in advance, or whatever actions of others he might use to advance his eternal plan, all of that is a giant leap from forcing anyone to do what is evil.

I know you're probably thinking about God hardening Pharaoh's heart and inciting David to sin, but there's more than meets the eye in those instances. We can talk at length about that, if you wish. What you must understand, however, is that no matter what strings God might be pulling behind the scenes, every angel and every human being is personally responsible for his own spiritual rebellion.

We angels often hear humans say that they're not sinners because they sin, but rather that they sin because they are sinners — which is as much to say that they can't help but sin. Yet Adam was no sinner by nature, and still he sinned. More importantly, Satan certainly was not created in a state of sin, but sinned nevertheless.

If you want to see that devilish line in its other usual disguises, how about these? "But I'm only human!" Or, "Nobody's perfect!" Yet Adam, though human, was created in a state of perfection, as was Satan. Even so, they both sinned because they had the capacity to choose between good and evil, right and wrong, obedience and rebellion, purity and sin — and chose wrongly. As do all who sin. Nobody sins out of compulsion or moral necessity, nor certainly because God wills it. If anyone's hoping to find someone else to blame, I'm sorry but everyone's on their own when it comes to sin. You can't even say (as

Eve did), "The devil made me do it." I'm afraid that's a line reserved exclusively for the devil himself, making one wonder how anyone could ever think that the Evil One was sent to Eden as a guardian cherub!

*a*re you saying it wasn't Satan being described by Isaiah and Ezekiel? Sorry, but I have to give you another of my "yes-and-no" answers. And this time mostly "no." But I understand why you ask. It's my mention of the guardian cherub, isn't it? As you know, Ezekiel describes in rather acerbic terms a mocking lament of a figure who looks for all intents and purposes as the Evil One — particularly for those who've already concluded that Isaiah's similar "funeral dirge" is also about the Evil One. But I can tell you with complete confidence that neither Isaiah nor Ezekiel was directing their respective prophecies against the Evil One. It wasn't cosmic history they were recording, but future events.[281]

In his mocking lament, Isaiah taunts the king of Babylon (indeed, by association, *all* of Babylon's kings), citing the king's imminent punishment for crimes committed against God's people. Babylon's king may think of himself as God's gift from heaven, but he is soon to find himself, like all men great and small, in a cruel grave. More especially, he will soon find himself in Sheol being taunted (in poetic depiction) by all the other pompous kings on whom God has pronounced a death sentence.

The personification of the king's demise is really a wider prophecy of the fall of Babylon itself. "I will cut off Babylon's name and descendants, says the Lord," Isaiah reports steely.[282]

---

281. Isaiah 14:12-15; Ezekiel 28:12-19
282. Isaiah 14:22

And, as if already completed, again comes Isaiah's portentous prediction of the destruction to come: "Babylon has fallen!"[283]

So the lament is not at all about the Evil One...apart from absolutely dripping with double-entendres, creating an intriguing interplay between the king of Babylon and the Evil One. Think of one, and you can almost see the other. Virtually everything Isaiah says regarding the king can be seen as an allusion to the Evil One. The details don't always fit nicely, but that's the nature of allusions. They're never meant to fit precisely, anymore than everything about Moses, Joshua, or David can be tied precisely to Jesus, though in all of them one can find meaningful allusions to the Christ they foreshadowed.

It hasn't helped your understanding for the King James Version gratuitously to insert the name *Lucifer* into Isaiah's prophecy, as that interpretation of "morning star" has fueled much of the speculation about the Evil One's identity in this lament. Nor has that speculation suffered from Isaiah's mention of the king's desire to make himself like the Most High God, since that's precisely what the Evil One also aspired to do. And then there's that obvious parallel between the Evil One's being hurled down to earth and the king's being cast down to Sheol.

In fact, the parallels extend even more interestingly to the destructive role each figure has played. Each in his own way, both the king of Babylon and the Evil One have "subdued nations," "struck down nations," and (don't you just love this one) "prevented their captives from returning home."[284] Paint a picture of one, and you could sell it to anyone hoping to buy a

---

283. Isaiah 21:9
284. Isaiah 14:6, 17

picture of the other! Call it a family resemblance, and you'd be about right.

What goes for Isaiah's mocking lament, goes also for Ezekiel's. Only the target of the scorn has changed, this time being the king of Tyre, that maritime city on the coast whose seaport and trade had made it wealthy...and proud. In its pride, Tyre (personified in its king) had thought itself as wise as a god, and, of course, economically invulnerable due to its rich trading empire. By some irony, Ezekiel prophesies that Tyre will be utterly destroyed by none other than Nebuchadnezzar, king of Babylon,[285] a nation itself destined to be destroyed as Isaiah had prophesied!

The stinging lament against Tyre and its king contains a double allusion: both to the Evil One and to Adam. Were they not both created perfect? Were they not both blameless until wickedness was found in them? Were they not both in Eden in the garden of God? Were they not both expelled from their natural home? And did they not both fall because of their desire to be as wise as God?[286] It's all there, isn't it? Instead of a two-for-one painting, this time you get a three-for-one special!

Again, not all of the details fit precisely. Neither the Evil One nor Adam was awash in precious jewels, as was Tyre. Or engaged in merchant trading. Or was reduced to rubble and ashes as nations looked on appalled. The lesson if ever there was one is that, no matter the specific details, all who follow in the Evil One's footsteps will come to the same end. A haughty spirit doesn't just go *before* a fall, it *causes* the fall!

---

285. Ezekiel 26:7
286. Ezekiel 28:1-2, 6

And about that reference to Tyre being a "guardian cherub" and present in the "garden in Eden," don't forget the figurative nature of the lament (complete with all those "fiery stones"). You yourself must have heard people talk about a place of extraordinary beauty as being "Paradise" or "Eden." It was no different with the people of Tyre at the height of its glory. They, too, thought they had reproduced the Garden of Eden on their lofty "mount of God" there on the coast. What's more, because of the city's commanding position as a commercial gateway, you can imagine how they would consider their thriving port as the "guardian cherub" of the trade routes. (Not unlike your own City of Angels, really.) As even common parlance will attest, at times allusions work both ways.

Let's go to the Garden...

*W*as the serpent in the Garden really Satan? That's a slightly qualified "yes." As you know, Satan is not explicitly mentioned in the Genesis 3 account, only the serpent. But there is an inseparable linkage between the two. If ever there were any doubt about the connection, you can read it for yourself in John's Revelation.[287] Depicting a great dragon in his apocalyptic vision, John pointedly speaks of *Satan*, the *devil*, and the ancient *serpent* as if all three are one and the same—represented collectively in the image of the dragon.

However, you must appreciate that Satan doesn't normally run around in a snake outfit any more than in a ludicrous red suit. Nor is he literally a serpent in any shape, form, or fashion. In the Garden, the Evil One took control of a living, breathing,

---

287. Revelation 12:7-12; 20:2

walking serpent and spoke through it in a way the serpent on its own could never have spoken, much like Balaam's famed donkey through which the spirit of the Lord spoke to Balaam.[288] You can also be sure that it wasn't future generations of that particular serpent's offspring who bear the spiritual brunt of the curse upon the Evil One they have now come to represent as they slither along the ground.[289] It was Satan himself, not the hapless serpent, who was the primary object of God's curse. That curse had nothing to do with Satan crawling on his belly and eating dust, but everything to do with the woman's son (Jesus) ultimately destroying the Evil One and all who would follow in his wicked footsteps.

But if serpents *could* talk, they'd be the first to tell you that nothing Satan controls emerges unscathed or unaffected. They might also suggest that, as with their once-erect progenitor in the Garden, it's the upright who have the most to fear from being brought low by the Evil One. So if you think you're standing secure, be extra careful that you do not fall.[290]

So the Garden of Eden was not just a myth story? Absolutely not. It's certainly no myth that the whole of Scripture speaks of the events in the Garden as historical fact.[291] Take Luke's genealogy of Jesus, for example. Not stopping at Abraham (as does Matthew's genealogy), Luke records the family tree all the way back to the first progenitor, Adam.[292] Real person. Real wife. Real serpent. Real trees. Real sin. So, yes, it was a real garden paradise—sadly now, also really gone in the post-Flood transformation of the primordial land masses.

---

288. Numbers 22:28-30
289. Luke 10:19
290. 1 Corinthians 10:12
291. Romans 5:12-14; 2 Corinthians 11:3; 1 Timothy 2:13-14
292. Matthew 1:1-17; Luke 3:23-38

But I suspect what you're really wanting to know is whether those classic conversations actually occurred, and the answer is that they did. It's through those conversations that you immediately start to see the difference between a providential, loving God and the degenerate Evil One. Whereas God generously permits Adam and Eve to eat from every tree in the Garden, barring only two, the serpent suddenly accentuates the negative, cynically asking if God really said they couldn't eat of those two trees — as if that were some onerous insult to them.

From the serpent's seemingly innocent question has arisen the now-standard protest: "That's not fair!" — the mantra of choice for self-willed libertines ever since. With but the slightest subtlety, the Evil One convinces Eve to question God's sovereign rule over her life. Who does God think he is? Dare he lay down rules for everyone but himself? (It was still that old *hierarchy* problem the Evil One had with God. That *submission* issue, that so miffed him.)

Abandoning all subtlety, the Evil One then just outright lies to Eve about the forbidden fruit *not* causing death. Despite his own prevarication, the Evil One infers it's *God* who is the liar! Can you believe it?

And for the *coup de grace* there's that line about "being like God," which, of course, reflected his own twisted ambition. Little did the Evil One appreciate how ironic his argument was. For man was already created *in the likeness of God*, and called to become more and more *like God* by rightly discerning between good and evil.[293] Man's sin would not be in *knowing* good from evil, but in *deciding for himself* what was good and

---

293. Romans 12:9, 21

what was not. By impudently assuming this exclusive attribute of deity, humankind would re-create themselves in the image of the Evil One, and become ever more like him.

As it happens, the Evil One actually ended up telling an unintended truth—that Eve's eyes would be opened if she ate the fruit. My, were they ever opened…to nakedness, shame, guilt, and regret! But by then it was too late to shove the by-then-slithering serpent back into his hole.

Far from being a myth story, the events in the Garden perfectly mirror your own personal "Garden," wherever it may be—albeit with no need for a talking serpent to entice you to partake of forbidden fruit. Once the first forbidden fruit was consumed, a Pandora's box of evil was opened wide for all time. The story of the Garden is the ongoing story of each person's individual rebellion and alienation. Yet, as seen even in the punishment meted out to man and serpent alike that day, it also brings with it the promise of reconciliation through submission, hope for despair, and life where there might only have been death. What could be more real than that?

*W*hat are we to make of the predicted conflict between offsprings? I take it you mean the second part of the curse against the serpent, in which God speaks of putting enmity between the woman's offspring and the serpent's.[294] By now I hope you are comfortable with the important role of primary applications and secondary allusions, for both play a part in the curse. (If you're musically minded, think *tones* and *overtones*.)

---

294. Genesis 3:15

First to the obvious, primary application. Eve's offspring, naturally, would be the entire human race. The serpent's offspring — or rather that of his alter-ego, the Evil One — would be Satan's evil angels. (He didn't *sire* them in any procreative sense, but they were certainly his progeny.) So the conflict is between humankind and the force of darkness unleashed by the Evil One. It is the ongoing conflict between "the world" (of which the Evil One is prince) and the godly realm of the Holy One. Between the true power of God and the faux power of Satan. Between one's allegiance to righteousness and one's allegiance to wickedness. Between one's love of good and one's love of evil. It's what Paul was talking about when he told King Agrippa of being commissioned to turn the Gentiles from darkness to light, and from Satan's power to God's.[295]

Yet how was that transformation to happen without the grace of God being bestowed through his beloved Son? Which brings us to the secondary allusion of the curse, foreshadowing the coming Savior of the world, "born of a woman."[296] This most special offspring would bring peace where there was enmity; harmony between God and man where once there was alienation. And although the Evil One would claim victory for the Son's death on the cross, the Son's very act of submission and servanthood would spell defeat for the one who had taken such offense at having to submit and serve. So it is that the Evil One would "strike the heel" of God's anointed, but at the end of the day his own head would be crushed. For the Evil One, the cross would be a miscalculated and Pyrrhic victory if ever there were one.

You humans sometimes speak of history repeating itself. There is a reassuring sense in which an already-crushed Satan

---

295. Acts 26:17-18; Colossians 1:13-14
296. Galatians 4:4

is crushed again each time God brings victory over your enemies. For example, the apostle Paul invoked the language of "Satan being crushed under your feet" when assuring the saints in Rome that those who were dividing and disrupting the church would soon be overcome. Paul's reference to Satan being crushed is not unlike what the Hebrew writer meant when he spoke of those who turned away from Christ as "crucifying him all over again."[297] It's not that the act itself is literally repeated, but that its spirit and essence is. Whether in Christ's death and resurrection or by every other victory God manifests in your own life, you can rest assured that Satan already *has been* crushed, even now *is being* crushed, and forever *will be* crushed!

Names, titles, and roles...

By what names is Satan properly known? As an adversary to both God and man, he is rightly called Satan.[298] You may find it as interesting as I do that when King David was reeling from false accusations being hurled in his direction, he prayed to God that some evil man be made a prosecutor of his enemies.[299] The word David chose for that prosecutor is "a satan," meaning *an adversary*, as in a court of law. There is delicious irony here. Not only is the chief adversary against God and the righteous an evil personage of the highest order, but he also ends up being the adversary of wicked men—who in their wickedness and slander mimic the very one who is out to destroy them! If misery loves company, so does evil.

---

297. Romans 16:20; Hebrews 6:6
298. Job 1:6-2:8; 1 Thessalonians 2:18
299. Psalm 109:6

Adding irony to irony, it's just such slander and false accusations that give rise to the name "devil," which means "to throw," as in—how do you say it—mudslinging? The connotations behind both "adversary" and "the devil" are so intertwined that the apostle Peter spoke of them interchangeably as "your adversary, the devil." (Or "Your enemy, the devil.")[300] Although you won't find the word *devil* in your Old Testament (except in some versions when the text is more properly referring to *demons*), you can find the devil's fingerprints all over the New Testament. Jesus calls him "devil" in his parables; John's gospel speaks of "the devil" entering Judas; Paul warns about "the devil's" schemes; and, of course, "the devil" features prominently in the Apocalypse.[301]

I find it fascinating that in your day and age it's not "Satan" but "the devil" who gets top billing in the minds of most— especially a disbelieving world. If perhaps an evil "Satan" would have to be taken more seriously, a caricatured devil in a red cape, complete with horns and a fork, can somehow be laughingly dismissed as a comedic figure. If only they knew the Evil One as I know him, they wouldn't be laughing....

Taking a page from his most notorious *modus operandi*, the devil is also rightly known as "the tempter." You can certainly appreciate how he got that name when you read about his temptation of Jesus in the desert. In but one brief account, the Evil One is called, "devil," "Satan," and "tempter."[302] Paul also speaks of him as "the tempter" when he fears that the disciples in Thessalonica might have fallen under the tempter's

---

300. 1 Peter 5:8
301. Matthew 13:38-39; Luke 8:12; John 13:2; Ephesians 6:11;
    Revelation 20:2
302. Matthew 4:1-11

influence.[303] (At some point, we have much to discuss about his powers of temptation.)

These household names are more familiar, of course, but not necessarily the most descriptive. As you could guess by now, I myself prefer to call him the Evil One, just as Jesus and the apostles often did.[304] Whatever else he is, first and foremost to me he will always be the very personification of evil and all things repugnant! But he has many names, and, rather perversely, seems to revel in all of them—even the ones you might think he'd loathe.

Call him a "roaring lion," for example, and the Evil One licks his chops.[305] Or a "dragon," and he loves how monstrously fearsome he must seem.[306] Call him a "murderer," and he proudly recounts his victims; or a "liar," and he'll look you straight in the eye and deny it. [307]

If you want to know what names the Evil One simply adores, it's all the ones that make him appear to be what he coveted when he instigated mutiny against the Holy One. How very pleased he is, for example, to be called a "king," and all the more so since that "king" is himself called by two names (*Abaddon*, in the Hebrew, and *Apollyon*, in the Greek) which mean *Destroyer*.[308] As I suggested earlier, it seems not to faze "the king" in the least that his only real kingdom is the cauldron Abyss of Tartarus!

---

303. 1 Thessalonians 3:5
304. Matthew 13:19, 38; John 17:15; Ephesians 6:16; 1 John 2:13-14; 3:12; 5:18-19
305. 1 Peter 5:8
306. Isaiah 51:9; Revelation 12:3-17; 20:2
307. John 8:44
308. Revelation 9:11

Naturally, the Evil One takes great pride in being the Prince of Demons; and the Ruler of the Kingdom of the Air (as he would insist they be capitalized).[309] And, oh, how he loves being known as the "prince of this world."[310] Yet for the Evil One it just doesn't get any better than being regarded as "the *god* of this age."[311] Despite being deliriously oblivious to the difference between the one true God and a cheap counterfeit, he can almost be heard shouting to the heavens: "Thank God, I'm God at last!"

Truth be known, the Evil One gets far more credit than he deserves. In his darkened, deluded mind, he may think he's achieved the position of power and authority he's craved so doggedly, but he has none of the respect owing to high position. Worse yet, his all-consuming pride and arrogance has so blinded him that he can't see just how weak and pitiful he really is.

Perhaps I shouldn't, but I happen to like the despicable name given to him by the Pharisees: "Beelzebub."[312] (Or Beelzebul, or Beelzeboul, if you prefer.) It's loosely derived from the Philistine god of Ekron, Baal-Zebub, whose name in its many variants means "lord of the dwelling," "lord of the flies," or "lord of filth."[313] If you imagine a stinking dung heap swarming with flies, you'll get the picture. Rather a telling snapshot of the Evil One, I'd say!

You may recall that, in writing to the saints in Corinth, Paul drew a sharp contrast between *believers and Christ* on one hand and *unbelievers and Belial* on the other.[314] Paul was talking about

---

309. Luke 11:15; Ephesians 2:2
310. John 12:31; 14:30; 16:11
311. 2 Corinthians 4:4
312. Matthew 12:22-28; Mark 3:22; Luke 11:14-20
313. 2 Kings 1:2
314. 2 Corinthians 6:15

lesson #5 pp. 180-183

the Evil One, of course, borrowing a term sometimes seen in the writings of his day. Paul's warning not to get mixed up with Belial and his followers is good advice, believe me. Don't ever think you can flirt with this "Belial" without being seduced.

come back to this lesson #10 pt. 2

*I*n what way is Satan the prince of the power of the air? It's one of those times when God takes what people mistakenly believe and reads into it truer meaning. In the first century, Jews as well as pagans believed that the atmosphere was thickly populated with all kinds of spiritual entities. In his letter to the saints in Ephesus, Paul draws on that belief to affirm the greater truth that the Evil One is the ruler of an evil kingdom about which they have only the foggiest notion—a kingdom where real, rather than imagined, spiritual beings do indeed operate in an unworldly dimension, both in and out of time and space.[315] Given human limitations, "air" is about as precise as Paul could be.

*W*hy did God allow Satan to inflict suffering on Job? Don't get me wrong, Satan has wreaked great havoc and human suffering by his belligerent behavior, but you must be careful as you read the story of Job, for that's what it truly is—a *story*. In terms of literary genre, the book of Job might best be described as a historical poem presenting fictional dialogue based on historical fact.

As Ezekiel would remind you, Job himself was a real-life historical figure, just like Noah and Daniel.[316] James, too, would testify that the notoriously patient Job was as real as you and

---

315. Ephesians 2:1-2
316. Ezekiel 14:14, 20

Angels, Demons, and the Devil

I.[317] Living during the time of the patriarchs, this unusually righteous man suffered a reversal of fortune few men have ever known, including the loss of his children, his great wealth, and even his health. Yet throughout the ordeal Job never once turned his back on God. By means of oral tradition, the story of Job was repeated generation after generation, such that "the patience of Job" became forever etched in the minds of the ancients.

That said, the *story* of Job's life which you have in your Bible was not reduced to writing until the time of the Exile, when Jews were questioning, not just in general why God allows suffering, but more particularly why the righteous suffer as well as the wicked. Not every Jewish knee had bowed to Baal! Yet along with those who had prostituted themselves to foreign gods, these innocent, righteous Jews had also been taken captive, lost all their worldly possessions, and suffered physically in quite unthinkable ways. The question weighing heavily on their minds was the timeless query: Why do bad things happen to good people? It was in response to this particularly stressful time in Israel's history that the book of Job was written, complete with its creative dialogue between God and Satan, and — far more so — between Job and his friends.

As the story of Job unfolds, Satan plays only a minor supporting role, setting up the theological conundrum of why God permits suffering, especially of the righteous. Once Satan plays his role in bringing about Job's losses and suffering, he fades completely out of the picture. Never after that opening scene is Satan indicted as the cause of man's suffering, or as the means whereby evil operates in the world. If you're familiar with the

---

317. James 5:11

story you know that, in the end, human suffering is tied to neither righteousness (which Job personally claimed) nor wickedness (as Job's friends argued), nor certainly to some nefarious forces of the Evil One. At the conclusion of the story, God strongly suggests to Job that there are certain profound questions which humans cannot possibly understand.

Would that I myself could give you an easy answer as to why humans suffer, but I have not been handed that brief, nor has any other angel. What I *can* tell you is that, in time, you will fully and completely understand the meaning behind the "problem" of human suffering.

In the meantime, you must not let the story of Job mislead you regarding the Evil One. If through some great tragedy you were to lose your loved ones, or become financially destitute, or even suffer great physical pain from some disease or disability, it would not be the work of the Evil One. (Nor likely God.) Unlike the story-line of Job, God and Satan aren't constantly testing you to see whose side you're on. Nor does God use Satan as his emissary to do harm. In the rare case that some adversity is demanded by the situation, we faithful angels are more than capable of carrying out that task ourselves.[318]

And there is also this caution. Unlike the impression you might get from the presence of Satan on two occasions when the angels are presenting themselves before God, you should not assume that these "angelic assemblies" necessarily took place in heaven, or even occurred at all. That we don't have *days* in heaven, as mentioned twice in the story,[319] should be a reminder of the fictional nature of the narrative. Same with

---

318. 2 Kings 19:35-36; Acts 12:23
319. Job 1:6-12; 2:1-7

that line about Satan roaming around the earth. All the debate among your scholars about what role Satan played in these angelic assemblies — whether as the Evil One, or perhaps simply as a benign celestial prosecutor — gets started on the wrong foot with a false assumption about these so-called "assemblies." And beware, particularly, of circular references to other so-called "assembly" passages when each is used artificially to prop up the others.

All of which is to say that the Evil One's role in the prelude to this classic piece of biblical literature owes its explanation to what Satan represents as an avowed opponent of God and all who are righteous. In the story itself, Satan is perfectly typecast in the role of the Accuser, who argues that Job's faithfulness to God was solely contingent upon his continued health and prosperity. Take away "the good life" from Job, Satan insists, and Job will renounce God in a heartbeat. Consistent with the Evil One's real-life rebellion against God, the Satan of the Job story slanders even God by suggesting that the Holy One is naively deluded about his "poster child," Job.

Your expression, "Fact is stranger than fiction" somehow comes to mind, though with an interesting twist. For in the story of Job the factual truth about the Evil One's malevolent character gives rise to the malevolent role he plays in the prelude to Job's exploration of the problem of suffering. Although the Evil One did not literally say or do what is attributed to Satan in the Job story, the fact is that it's exactly what he *might* have said and done, given the opportunity. It's a role the Evil One certainly would have relished!

Speaking of the Devil

- to Go Back to p. 141

*H*ow are we to understand Zechariah's vision of Satan? Perhaps it's best to think of it as a variation on theme from the story of Job in the sense that it's not an account to be taken literally. However, rather than its being a piece of historical fiction, what the prophet Zechariah sees at the end of the Babylonian exile in 520 B.C. is a vision (the fourth of eight) in which Satan appears with "the angel of the Lord" and Joshua the high priest.[320] It was *this* Joshua (not Moses' successor) who, along with Zerubbabel the governor, was even then leading the Jewish exiles back to Jerusalem. As we've already discussed, the "angel of the Lord" in this instance is no ordinary angel, but a pre-incarnation manifestation of the Son. Yet this particular appearance of the "angel of the Lord" is not an actual appearance of the Son, as in other accounts, only an envisioned one. The same goes for Joshua and Satan. Don't forget, it's a *vision*! Just as easily, it could have been a dream.

As in the story of Job, Satan's role in Zechariah's vision is true to form. Once again, Satan is depicted as God's evil adversary, this time personifying the opposition being brought against God's promised restoration of Jerusalem and the temple, and the revival of Israel's priesthood—represented here in the person of Joshua. Just as in the book of Job, Satan's minor role quickly fades as the vision moves on to describe how the priesthood was to be purified of its sins and the nation restored in holiness. The point of the vision? Evil will not triumph over good! God's master plan will not be thwarted by any force, either from your world or ours—least of all from the Evil One.

Want to know what I like most about Zechariah's vision? It's that wonderful line about the coming servant of God ("the

---

320. Zechariah 3:1-10

Branch") while, *right there in the vision*, "the angel of the Lord" was himself that very Branch! Just how sweet is that?

How the devil operates...

Was it Satan or God who incited David to sin? I knew you'd come back to this question! And who hasn't, if they've read both 2 Samuel 24 and 1 Chronicles 21?[321] The seeming conflict has both an easy answer and a more complex one. The easy answer is supplied by James, who rightly assures you that God isn't in the business of tempting his creatures to sin.[322] Not, not, not; never, never, never. So you can take it at face value that whatever was intended by the words "God incited David" had nothing to do with *tempting* David to sin.

That's where it gets complicated, but not *that* complicated. Surely you recall that marvelous line from Joseph to his brothers as they cowered before him thinking their heads were about to roll for having sold him into slavery. To their great relief, they suddenly hear their brother saying, "You fully intended to do me harm, but God intended your evil for good in order to accomplish his own eternal will."[323]

You have a funny expression, I believe. Something about "taking lemons and making lemonade"? Well, that's sort of what I'm talking about here. David's decision to take a census against God's will was his own foolish idea for which he bore

---

321. 2 Samuel 24:1-10; 1 Chronicles 21:1-7
322. James 1:13
323. Genesis 50:20

146

full responsibility — as he himself readily admitted.[324] But God in his sovereign providence used David's sin as an occasion to punish, not just David, but all of Israel, whose sins begged divine judgment.

In that sense — but in that sense alone — it could be said that God "incited" David to do the census. Hebrew writers weren't always the greatest at distinguishing between primary and secondary causes. Since God is the ultimate cause of the universe, to them it was as if God was the cause of everything. Ultimately, of course, God as Creator is the First Cause of all things, so attributing all things to a sovereign God is the right idea. But that alone doesn't account for secondary causes which God allows but does not initiate. God is not the author of sin.

It's another discussion altogether, but you can see this same dynamic at work when "God hardened Pharaoh's heart," especially when you can also read that Pharaoh and his officials "hardened their own hearts."[325] This dynamic also explains how Rehoboam's sin against Israel could be described as a "turn of events from God."[326] God takes man's "lemons" and turns them into "lemonade" for the advancement of his eternal plan. If you've ever wondered how God does that, sometimes he just sets the stage so that a given actor can walk on and act out whatever role he himself has chosen to play. At other times, to change the metaphor, God just waits and picks up the pieces of a broken life, then glues them back together. But he never compels, never coerces, never dictates.

"So what about Satan's role?" you ask. That, too, is less straight-forward than it might seem. Naturally, tempting and

---

324. 2 Samuel 24:10; 1 Chronicles 21:8
325. Exodus 9:12, 34-35
326. 2 Chronicles 10:15

inciting is right down Satan's alley. But the glaring omission of any mention of Satan in the earlier of the two accounts of this episode should at least raise a question in your mind as to whether the Evil One actually played a role in prompting David's sin, or perhaps was cited in the later account for another reason altogether.

Have you ever wondered why David's census was so odious in God's eyes, considering that God himself had demanded a similar census on two prior occasions?[327] Or why, out of the hundreds of sins recorded in the Old Testament, only this one is associated with the name *Satan*? The answer to both questions lies in the motive David had for ordering this particular census.

One of the unstated reasons for the earlier two censuses (the ones God ordered) was to highlight the fact that Israel's victories would not be due to their overwhelming numbers, but attributable alone to the power of God. David's census (the one God judged as evil) had just the opposite rationale. Instead of reflecting Israel's dependence on God, the census was meant as a display of national pride in Israel's military might. With that many soldiers on your side, who needs God?

Had you confronted David about that, he would have flatly denied it. But his leading commander, Joab, was not fooled in the least, and tried in vain to dissuade David from his folly. Because he found David's order repulsive, Joab staged his own private protest by not including Levi and Benjamin in the numbering. He was not about to inflate David's ego and pride any more than necessary.

---

327. Numbers 1:1-3; 26:1-3

Is it becoming clear now why the name *Satan* was attached to David's sin? What David was motivated by — *incited by* — was Satan-like pride! In this instance (as in others as well), "Satan" is being used metaphorically. When someone says, "The devil's got in him," or "The devil made him do it," nobody takes it literally. It's just that whatever's been done has a devilish quality to it.

It's not exactly the same, but remember when Jesus referred to having seen Satan fall from heaven?[328] If you recall, Jesus makes that statement in response to the seventy-two specially-commissioned disciples who returned to him so euphoric about having cast out demons. Lest they become too proud of themselves in their celebrations, Jesus points them to the very picture of pride causing one's downfall. That picture was of Satan.

To update the metaphor, if one of your modern computers had a software program called "Pride" installed, the icon you'd likely click on would be an image of Satan and a lightning bolt. When what you're talking about is pride, all you need say is *Satan*. The words *Satan* and *pride* are practically synonymous.

This personification of pride also explains Paul calling his thorn in the flesh a "messenger from Satan."[329] Why did God send this "thorn" to Paul? "To prevent my becoming conceited," Paul acknowledges in the wake of his having been honored with a sneak preview of the Other Side. Though Paul had pleaded with God to take away his "thorn," Paul fully appreciated the role it played in reminding him of the pitfalls of the conceit so dramatically personified by the Evil One.

---

328. Luke 10:17-20
329. 2 Corinthians 12:7-10

It's no surprise, then, that Paul would warn against appointing recent converts as church leaders, lest they become conceited and fall under the same judgment as the Evil One.[330] A novice disciple given leadership responsibility might well attach more importance to himself than is rightly due. No fancy explanations are needed. All Paul has to do is mention the devil, and immediately we know he's talking about a problem with pride.

At the end of the day, it was David's pride alone that prompted him to sin. But the Evil One would have pinned a medal on him; and — more importantly — God himself used David's sin as a means of carrying out his own divine plan.

*D*oes this also explain Jesus' rebuke to Peter? Well, sort of, if you're referring to the time when Jesus rounded on Peter, saying, "Get behind me, Satan!" What you're sensing correctly is that Jesus invoked the name *Satan* merely as a metaphor, not intending to say that Peter himself *was* Satan, or that Satan was somehow speaking through Peter. Yet, on this particular occasion the *Satan* metaphor did not have reference to *pride*, although Peter's hutzpa in taking Jesus aside and reproving him lets you know that Peter was not overly suffering from humility. But that's not what Jesus had in mind. This time, the metaphor stood for Satan as a *tempter*.

Peter's censure of Jesus followed in the wake of Jesus telling the apostles he would soon be killed by the Jewish establishment.[331] Along with the other apostles, Peter still had a blurred understanding about the spiritual nature of Jesus' Messiahship. How

---

330. 1 Timothy 3:6
331. Matthew 16:21-23

was Jesus' Messianic *revolution* to take place, Peter wondered, if Jesus was already throwing in the towel? (Had Peter not been listening when Jesus assured them he would rise again on the third day!)

For Jesus (already contemplating the horrific death he must face on the cross), Peter's stinging reprimand was not just an unwarranted chastisement, but a temptation to cut and run. More than that, it was a temptation to accomplish his mission the easy way—by divine fiat rather than by human submission. Wasn't that what Satan had tempted Jesus to do during their confrontation in the wilderness? No wonder Satan came instantly to Jesus' mind when Peter unwittingly became a stumbling block to Jesus' firm resolve. What Peter said could have come directly out of Satan's own mouth!

*D*id Jesus speak metaphorically about Satan wanting to "sift" Peter? No, not this time. Apart from derailing Jesus' own ministry, nothing would have pleased the Evil One more than shaking the faith of Jesus' apostles. Remember, this was taking place at a time when the Evil One was permitted free access to Jesus and his apostles.

And it wasn't just Peter whom Jesus was warning, but the Twelve—all of whom had just been quarreling about who among them was the greatest. Using a plural term, Jesus warned: "Satan has asked to sift you *all*."[332] (Even if it turned out to be Judas, not Peter, one out of twelve is a pretty respectable capture ratio, is it not?)

---

332. Luke 22:31-32

*H*ow involved was Satan in Judas' betrayal? Very!
And Jesus knew it all along. Remember when he was
speaking to the Twelve and said — as if out the blue —
"One of you is a devil!"?[333] Naturally, Jesus didn't mean Judas
was *the* devil, or was *possessed* by the devil. But Jesus knew in
advance that Judas would be doing the devil's work for him.

That Jesus would appoint his own betrayer as one of the
twelve apostles might surprise you, but not me. Not looking
back on the Evil One himself. God created him too, knowing
in advance that the Evil One would rebel. (As he did *you*, if I
may say so, along with all of humankind.)

Judas and the Evil One shared something in common: a spirit
of betrayal. Moreover, the Evil One's pride and Judas' greed
were first cousins in the family of sins. Indeed, the connections
just keep coming, with the Evil One being a liar and a murderer and Judas being a thief and an accomplice to murder.[334]
So the Evil One certainly chose the right partner in crime.

Behind the scenes, the Evil One was orchestrating Christ's crucifixion by creating opportunities and making all the right connections for Judas to play a crucial role in the unthinkable
horror he would find himself committing, ultimately to his
great chagrin. Up until the very last, Judas was tortured by the
prospect of what he was about to do, having to convince himself of the rightness of the cause in order to justify his greed.
Hadn't Jesus already betrayed the apostles by not marching into
Jerusalem and setting up a government of which they would be
heads? Hadn't Jesus already betrayed the people by not accept-
ing the mantle of kingship they were so anxious to place on his
shoulders? Surely it's not treason to betray a betrayer!

---

333. John 6:70-71
334. John 8:44; 12:4-6

As the evening meal was being served in the upper room, Judas was wound as tight as a spring. By then he had passed the point of no return. The Evil One had won the day. It was only a matter of carrying out the plan.[335] When talk of a betrayer began going around the table, Judas put on an act worthy of the Evil One himself. "Surely it's not I, Rabbi," Judas said ever so innocently (yet not daring to look Jesus in the eye).[336] But Jesus knew. And so did Judas. The moment Jesus handed Judas the bread he had dipped into the common bowl, Judas all but invited the Evil One to share both his bread and his treachery. From that point on, Judas was irretrievably in league with the devil. Just as when Judas first decided to conspire with the chief priests, once again the Evil One entered Judas as surely as if Judas were possessed![337]

id Satan enter into Ananias in the same way? Not exactly, but close. What Ananias (and his wife Sapphira) had in common with Judas was greed and deception.[338] Anytime you have that connection, you might as well attribute it to the Evil One, because from the very beginning he has inspired all deception. Whenever the sin of deception enters your heart, you become the offspring of the father of lies[339] — even if you happen to be a child of God by adoption. The Evil One himself doesn't literally enter into the heart, but his patented wickedness does!

Some special cases...

---

335. John 13:2
336. Matthew 26:20-25; Mark 14:17-21
337. Matthew 26:14; Luke 22:1-6; John 13:21-27
338. Acts 5:1-6
339. John 8:44; Acts 13:9-10

*W*hat more can you say about Jesus' temptation in the wilderness? Since I was an eye-witness, virtually everything.... As I earlier mentioned in passing, several of us angels were assigned by the Father to protect the Son from the wild animals there in that deserted plain. However, our orders were strictly limited to physical, not spiritual, protection. Jesus was on his own when it came to being tempted. (Nor, I assure you, did we slip him any food during those forty days of fasting.)

I know that many, if not most, who read the account of Jesus' face-to-face encounter with the Evil One look to that confrontation as an example of human temptation and the best strategy for overcoming it.[340] There is much to be said for that conclusion, including the importance of using Scripture to counter whatever temptation presents itself. And I suppose if one tries hard enough, it's possible to find the traditional three temptations: lust of the eyes, lust of the flesh, and the pride of life. During his lifetime, Jesus certainly experienced all three types of temptation—and overcame each one.[341] But that's not what the desert encounter was all about.

You should have heard the supercilious sneer in the Evil One's voice when he kept repeating, "*If* you are the Son of God...." The Evil One knew good and well that Jesus was the Son of God! That wasn't the issue. The issue was whether Jesus' fleshly incarnation was only a pretense. If you think about it, none of Jesus' temptations there in the desert are temptations you yourself face. Ever been tempted to turn a stone into bread? (And would it be a sin if you did?) Ever been tempted

---

340. Matthew 4:1-11; Mark 1:12-13; Luke 4:1-13
341. Hebrews 4:15

to jump off the tallest building around and hope that we angels would catch you? See where I'm headed on this?

The Evil One knew that Jesus — being the Son of God — could turn a rock into bread as easily as turning water into wine...*if he acted as the Son of God*. And the Evil One certainly knew that we angels would keep Jesus from harm should he for any reason fall from the highest pinnacle of the temple...*if* Jesus chose to rely on his divinity to save him in every instance. Most of all, the Evil One knew that all the world's kingdoms would easily be within Jesus' grasp...*if* Jesus conquered them by divine fiat. (It certainly wouldn't have happened by bowing down to the Evil One!)

So the question hanging in the balance was whether, when truly tempted in human ways rather than as the Son of God, Jesus would use his divinity as a crutch to overcome those temptations. Aren't you yourself tempted to think that Jesus remained sinless *because he was God*? But if that's the case, then his "overcoming temptation" would have been a sham and a farce! If the only reason Jesus was able to conquer sin is because he was the divine Son of God, then he wasn't really tempted like you are tempted. How then could his experience help you in any way?[342]

When all is said and done, Jesus' temptation in the wilderness was not about *Jesus*, but about *you*! Don't you see? Jesus refused to use his divinity as a crutch so as to rob *you* of any temptation to use your *humanity* as an excuse for your own sin. He was not perfect *as the Son of God*. He was perfect *as the Son of Man*! Now do you understand what Jesus meant when

---

342. Hebrews 2:18

he said, "Be perfect, as your Father in heaven is perfect"?[343] No more excuses! No more saying, "But nobody's perfect." No more thinking, "But I'm only human!"

Oh yes, I know your next question. If that's the case, you ask, why is Jesus the only human never to have sinned? The answer is that Jesus knew unequivocally *who he was* and acted accordingly. He knew he was not *just* human, but also the Son of God. Which is a clue to your own path to overcoming sin. If at the first sign of temptation you remembered *whose you are* — and acted accordingly — there's not a temptation in the world that could conquer you.

What's more, if you are in Christ, then you too are a son (or daughter) of God. You've been made for finer things than sin. Maybe you can't turn stones into bread or water into wine, but I dare say you can do a lot better than you're doing to overcome temptation. Telling yourself that you're only human is the quickest way I know to cave in to it. You might as well just shout to the heavens, "I can't help myself! I can't help myself!" But we both know better than that.

Sorry, but sometimes I get carried away. From my celestial vantage point, I do sorely grieve at all the unworthy rationalizing I witness on earth — especially since the Son went to such great lengths to prevent it.

*D*oes Satan ever contribute to moral or spiritual reform? Indirectly, of course, Satan plays an important role in reminding humankind of what *not* to become. His striking character is put out there for everyone to

---

343. Matthew 5:48

see...and avoid! Similar to how Jesus personifies righteous-ness, the Evil One—though not incarnate as Jesus was incar-nate—is the quintessential example of all that is evil.

Yet I expect you're asking me something more specific. Am I right? And does it have to do with the discipline of wayward believers? I thought so. I'm often asked what Paul meant in his first Corinthian letter when he directed the disciples in Corinth to hand over to Satan the sexually immoral man in their midst so that his sin might be destroyed and his soul saved on the Day of Judgment.[344] I'm also asked about Paul's enigmatic reference to his handing Hymenaeus and Alexander over to Satan to be taught not to blaspheme.[345] In the first case, there was a problem with morality; in the second, the problem was with doctrinal error. Yet in each instance, Paul hoped for real reform by "delivering these individuals to Satan."

Rather obviously, Paul was not expecting the Evil One to take those fellows in tow and teach them the way of the Lord more perfectly. The Evil One doesn't run a reform school! But the Evil One does have a way of bringing people to their knees when they finally come to grips with the disaster that invari-ably results from following in his footsteps of pride and de-ception. It was not just sexual sin that beset the immoral man in Corinth, but his arrogant audacity in thinking he could con-tinue to be part of God's holy body while living a life of open moral rebellion. (Even the disciples there in Corinth had a rather perverse pride about their "liberally-minded, loving Christian tolerance"!)

And it was not blasphemy of the usual kind of which Hy-menaeus and Alexander were guilty, but the kind of doctrinal

---

344. 1 Corinthians 5:1-5
345. 1 Timothy 1:18-20

heresy that entails blasphemy. (This is the special blasphemy committed by those whose teachings ultimately assail the very nature and character of God.)

In both instances, showing them out the door (or dismissing them from the table, as it were) would give opportunity for them to see the error of their ways and do an about-face. What Paul was counting on was a reservoir of spiritual conscious- ness that would respond favorably to tough love. For all those self-righteous people who think they are spiritual when they are not, treating them as you would treat the Evil One can often bring them back to their senses. Unfortunately, it doesn't always work. Sometimes there's simply not enough moral consciousness (or humility) to draw from. (You might be sur- prised to know that prompting moral reform is usually easier than humbling the proud.)

The good news, as I expect you already know, is that the immoral man in Corinth took a hard look at himself in the mirror, saw the despicable image of the Evil One, and turned his life around.[346] As have countless others who have experienced the tough love of disassociation from their fellow believers. Although everyone acts like the Evil One from time to time, few can stand being os- tracized as if they were Satan himself in the flesh.

*D*id Satan really stop Paul from going to Thessa- lonica? On one level, yes. Naturally, Paul could have overcome any obstacle the Evil One put in his way. Rest assured that the power of God within Paul was greater than anything the Evil One could have thrown in his

---

346. 2 Corinthians 2:5-11

path. But the opposition that the Evil One orchestrated in Corinth—particularly in the synagogue—left Paul with little choice but to abandon his plans to visit the Thessalonians.[347] It was right and proper, then, for Paul to blame the Evil One.[348] By contrast, when the Holy Spirit kept Paul from entering into Asia on his second mission trip, and—more specifically—when the Spirit of Jesus prevented Paul from entering Bithynia, we're talking about direct intervention. As with Jonah before him, in these two instances Paul really had no choice whatsoever. It was God's means of preparing the way for calling Paul to Macedonia instead.[349] Only the Holy One has the power of direct intervention, not the Evil One.

How would you explain Satan binding that crippled **woman for eighteen years?** Oh, to be sure, Satan has exercised real power within the boundaries of time and circumstance set by the Holy One. In the specific case you're asking about, the woman whom Jesus healed had been crippled all those years *by a spirit*—which is to say by a possessing demon.[350] No need to go into all of that just now. I'm sure you'll have plenty of questions to ask about demons. But I'll just say for the moment that there is an inseparable connection between demons and the Evil One. They are his operatives, his henchmen. They do his dirty work. So when Jesus said that the poor woman was Satan's victim, he was telling it like it is.

---

347. Acts 18:5-11
348. 1 Thessalonians 2:17-18
349. Acts 16:6-10
350. Luke 13:10-15

Angels, Demons, and the Devil

Lessons from the Lord...

*a*re humans ever Satan's operatives? All the time. But not in the same way as demons. (See, you keep pushing me to talk about demons, don't you!) Whereas demons are the Evil One's personal thugs answering specifically to his orders, humans are unwitting instruments who do the Evil One's bidding without always being aware of it. Wittingly or unwittingly, when they fall for lies promulgated by the Evil One and live their lives accordingly, they are advancing the cause of evil. In fact, sometimes humans do such a good job of furthering the Evil One's agenda that he just sits back and takes a day off!

Consider false teachers, for example. When they spew out their heresies and deception, they join the ranks of the rebels who took part in the Great Uprising. (Of course, most false teachers would never in a million years admit to being a false teacher, or even recognize it in themselves. Some do, but that's another story.)

As strange as it may seem, even the most overtly corrupt false teachers (those who peddle the gospel for profit) appear to their audiences as angels of light, or messengers of enlightenment. In that, they mimic the one they serve, who has always carried off the same hypocritical charade with such great flair.[351] Merely consider the Evil One's triumphant *tour de force* in the Garden of Eden. Who would have suspected there was such a sinister creature behind that drippingly sweet voice of the serpent?

Never forget that the one you imitate is the one you serve. Whose servant are you?

---

351. 2 Corinthians 11:13-15

*I*s this what Jesus was talking about in his parable of the weeds? Precisely. In the parable, the farmer sows good seed in his field but soon discovers to his horror that weeds are growing up among the grain.[352] Seems his enemy had snuck in when the farmer wasn't looking and planted bad seed. As Jesus explains the parable, the enemy is none other than the Evil One. And who are the weeds? The *sons* of the Evil One. Evil begets evil. From Jesus' own lips you can hear confirmation that Satan has human as well as supernatural operatives. The unrighteous (not demons this time!) are doing much of the damage that the Evil One intends.

But never forget the ending to the story. There's a great harvest coming, and we angels will be sent to gather up all these "weeds" and throw them into a burning furnace where they will be consumed. Like father, like "son"![353]

Although Jesus didn't specifically mention the Evil One in his parable of the net, all the same things apply.[354] Just like "the weeds," the unrighteous "bad fish" who live alongside the righteous "good fish" in this life will be doing some major weeping and wailing as they are unceremoniously thrown into hell's destructive fire along with the Evil One whose wicked cause they serve. He who has ears to hear, and all that....

*H*ow are we to understand Satan's role in the parable of the sower? As you know, when Jesus interprets the parable, he identifies the Evil One as the one responsible for the seed falling along the path being eaten

---

352. Matthew 13:24-43
353. Matthew 25:41
354. Matthew 13:47-50

by the birds — which is to say that Satan is responsible for short-lived conversions.[355] One might think Jesus would also have attributed the other examples of falling away to the Evil One as well, but, surprisingly, Jesus puts those failures down to persecution, worries, and wealth. So why associate Satan only with the birds, or why associate him with *birds* at all? The reason becomes clear to anyone familiar with the Judaic literature in Jesus' day. In a number of extrabiblical writings, Satan was associated with birds destructively eating the seed planted by farmers. By making the same association in his parable, Jesus instantly reaches his audience with something familiar they can relate to. If they can visualize Satan as birds destroying a crop before it ever really gets started, they can understand how growth of God's kingdom is hindered from the very start by a sinful world emanating from the Evil One. Had Jesus chosen to do so, he could also have attributed to Satan even persecution, worries, and wealth, since they all play into the Evil One's masterplan.

Mind control...

*A*re idle minds truly the devil's workshop? I have to admit I've always thought that to be a funny expression, something on par with how many angels can dance on the head of a pin. If you think about it, *active minds* can also be the devil's workshop! Minds filled with lust, minds seriously contemplating harm, minds busily dreaming up schemes to cheat and defraud. But I appreciate the sentiment lying behind the expression. Minds that are not engaged in positive thought do lend themselves more easily to negative

---

355. Matthew 13:1-9, 18-23; Mark 4:1-9, 13-20; Luke 8:4-8, 11-15

thought. Worse yet, minds that are not engaged at all create a vacuum for the Evil One to fill.

Not that the Evil One literally invades one's mind and starts doing the thinking himself. That has more to do with possession than influence, with a *house* rather than a *workshop*. But an idle mind is certainly more vulnerable to the schemes of the Evil One encompassed by his Grand Strategy to corrupt humankind and enlist you in the Rebellion. If one is not actively thinking about good things to do, he's more likely by far to be thinking up something bad to do. And isn't that just exactly what the Evil One would have wanted!

*D*oes Satan set traps for us? Not exactly like you set traps for vermin, or like the police set up their diabolical speed traps (so I'm told!). Not once but twice, the apostle Paul used the word *trap* when instructing his young protégé Timothy. In his first letter, Paul instructed Timothy to appoint local church leaders who had a good reputation in the community, lest in disgrace they fall into "the devil's trap."[356] While you might imagine the Evil One stealthily lying in wait with baited trap in order to catch some unsuspecting church leader, don't overlook the detail that the disgrace *precedes* the trap—not the other way around. The trap of which Paul speaks is the shameful trap that the Evil One himself fell into when he so disgraced himself. Don't fall into the same trap as the devil, Paul warns!

In his second letter to Timothy, Paul nudges closer to speaking of a spring-loaded trap that takes its victims captive.[357] The

---

356. 1 Timothy 3:7
357. 2 Timothy 2:22-26

"victims" in this case are those who give themselves over to rancorous quarreling and foolish arguing—even about spiritual matters. A church leader who constantly picks fights with his brothers over doctrinal issues of all sorts and lambasts everyone who disagrees with him has fallen into a trap worthy of the Evil One's greatest plots. That's exactly how the Evil One would like spiritual leaders to act. Far from earnestly contending for the faith, as they suppose, their contentiousness only furthers the agenda of the Evil One.[358] Unless they repent, they will remain captives, not couriers.

How about Satan's schemes? You mean, does he actually go around scheming against man? From the very beginning, he certainly *has*! And he keeps on doing it at every opening he's given. Clearly, Paul was not unaware of Satan's original battle plan, which is why he urged the Corinthians to forgive repentant sinners so that they not be outwitted by the Evil One.[359]

"The devil's schemes" is also what Paul identified for the Ephesians as the enemy they were to fight against.[360] It's one thing to go to war against some visible enemy. At least you have some idea of their strategy, even if they are terrorists rather than traditional armies. With the Evil One, you're dealing with a battle plan devised by an invisible enemy—the powers of darkness and spiritual forces who once inhabited the heavenly realms and have wielded more power than any earthly enemy. That battle plan of evil includes sneak attacks, diversions, subterfuge, and psychological warfare. In a world of constant

---

358. Jude 1:3
359. 2 Corinthians 2:5-11
360. Ephesians 6:10-17

conflict between the Holy One's divine plan of redemption and the Evil One's diabolical plan of rebellion, one must always be on "red alert."

Yet the picture Paul paints of spiritual warfare has less to do with the Evil One's specific schemes against specific individuals and more to do with your own strategy to overcome sin. For example, when Paul warns against "giving the devil a foothold," he's not suggesting that the devil is in some general way, minute by minute, "out to get you."[361] (Nor certainly *you* in particular!) In this particular instance, Paul is talking specifically about the evil of anger. If you let your simmering anger spill over to the next day, as it were, you play into the Evil One's master plan. Anger, resentment, grudges, and long-standing feuds are all on Satan's wish list for man. They are all acts of rebellion against God.

*I*s Satan concerned about unbelievers? Not as long as they remain unbelievers! His greatest hope is that they come nowhere near to having faith. And to keep that from happening he's introduced evil into the world to lure away the gullible and spiritually lazy. Is there something that deceives? It is of the Evil One. Or perhaps something that sounds right but couldn't be more wrong? Give Satan the credit! His alluring world of evil has captivated and blinded all those who are blithely stumbling down the road to perdition.[362]

Don't be fooled that somehow this is all a part of God's own plan. If you are a serious student of the Word, you are well aware of the conundrum where God is said to send a powerful delusion so that unbelievers will believe the Evil One's lies

---

361. Ephesians 4:26-27
362. 2 Corinthians 4:4

rather than acknowledge the truth. But don't forget it's a truth which they themselves have already freely rejected.[363] It is the unbeliever, unprompted by God, who has fallen for all the counterfeit miracles and other deceptions promulgated by the Evil One (as applies equally to the lawless one—Satan's "bag man" — of whom Paul spoke in his second letter to the Thessalonians.[364])

So why does God *need* to send unbelievers a powerful delusion? He doesn't. It's just that when someone chooses falsehood over truth, God does nothing to stop him, and indeed permits that person to be totally consumed in error. Error is always a powerful, captivating delusion—as most people have experienced at some point in their lives. Indeed, *every* believer was once enmeshed in Satan's world of evil.[365] Merely consider your own life. No offense, but you know as well as I that you once lived a worldly life, giving in to fleshly cravings and embarrassing thoughts. And I don't have to tell you that, even after committing your life to Christ, old habits die hard. Perseverance on *your part*, and—far more so—grace on *God's part*, is the only road ahead. But praise God that you who were once dead in your unbelief are now alive by faith in Christ! (If that truly applies to you....)

*C*an believers ever fall back into Satan's clutches? Absolutely. Why else all the warnings in Scripture? "Be careful lest you fall."[366] "Be careful lest there be found in you a heart of unbelief, in departing from God."[367]

---

363. 2 Thessalonians 2:9-11
364. 2 Thessalonians 2:1-12
365. Ephesians 2:1-2
366. Deuteronomy 4:9, 23; 11:6; Luke 21:34; 1 Corinthians 10:12
367. Hebrews 3:12-15

Paul could not have been clearer on this point when talking about the need for young widows to keep themselves pure. Remember what he said? "Some have already turned away to follow in Satan's footsteps."[368] Likewise, Peter reckoned that certain false teachers plaguing the church had escaped the corruption of the world by knowing Jesus Christ, only to be entangled in it all over again. They had become worse off than ever.[369] The distasteful images Peter invokes describe a dog returning to his vomit and a freshly-washed pig going back and wallowing in the mud!

It's one thing to have confidence that Christ himself will never let you down. About that, you can be absolutely, positively certain. The work he accomplished on the cross continues even now to protect you from the Evil One.[370] The very reason the Son came to earth was to destroy the devil's work![371] But Christ doesn't promise to protect you from yourself. The same door that bars the Evil One from snatching you away in the dead of night is a door that you yourself have the freedom to walk out through, should you be so foolish to do so.

Can I share with you something I find interesting along these lines? I know that many followers of Christ sincerely believe in what is often termed "once saved, always saved" — that it's impossible for a truly saved person to lose his salvation. I can appreciate the concern for the believer's eternal security, especially looking at it from the standpoint of God's faithfulness. But what intrigues me is how often these same people speak so fervently about the urgency for spiritual warfare against the Evil One *as if* one could really and truly fall away under Satan's sway and be lost. If at the end of the day it's impossible to be

---

368. 1 Timothy 5:14-15
369. 2 Peter 2:20-22
370. John 17:15; 2 Thessalonians 3:3; 1 John 5:18
371. 1 John 3:8

lost, how could the Evil One be a serious threat to any saved believer?

Since even the saved sin, does that mean the saved are "of Satan"? Yes...*when they sin.* If that seems an inconvenient truth, it is truth nevertheless. John made that perfectly clear in his first epistle when he said that whoever sins is of the devil.[372] Which is to say that *sin itself* is devilish, satanic, and evil—invariably mimicking the Evil One, who out of all creation was the first to sin.

Please hear me carefully. If you continue to sin even after being saved, it doesn't mean you are suddenly *unsaved.* What it does mean is that you must take your sin far more seriously than you do. It means that when you sin you are *acting* as if you are of Satan rather than of God. It means that if you wish to remain true to your Christian commitment you must quit sinning. Seriously, *quit sinning!*[373]

If you are a child of God, sin is beneath you. If you are a follower of Christ, sin betrays your loyalty. If you are supposed to be a shining light to the world, sin darkens your Christian witness. Even an unbelieving world intuitively knows that being free from a life of sin ought to be the bright-line difference between children of God and children of the Evil One.[374]

Yet I fear that my saying "life of sin" lets you off the hook too easily. It has the ring of a dyed-in-the-wool reprobate, not a Bible-believing, church-going, praying believer who happens

---

372. 1 John 3:8
373. 1 John 3:9
374. 1 John 3:10

to sin from time to time. Am I right? Unfortunately, you are the very kind of sinner John had in mind. He wasn't talking about those who commit robbery, rape, and murder, but about those who don't love their own brothers and sisters in Christ. If by any chance you're having a problem doing that, then you belong to the Evil One just as much as Cain, who killed his brother.[375] There's more than one way to "kill" a brother. And more than one way to "belong to the Evil One" who was the first to commit "murder."[376]

Still wondering how a saved child of God can be "of the devil" through ongoing sin? Strange as it sounds, it's because you *have* overcome the Evil One that you *must* overcome the Evil One![377] What I find odd is not that saved children of God *can* be of the devil (who himself once was perfect), but that saved children of God would ever continue to *act like* they're of the devil.

*I*n what way is the world under Satan's control? Certainly not in any ultimate sense. Never fear, the Holy One is still absolutely and positively in control! When John said that the whole world is under the control of the Evil One, he wasn't suggesting for a moment that the Evil One is in charge of the earth.[378] John is simply highlighting the contrast between those who are children of God and those who live their lives under the influence of the Evil One.

Those who are worldly comprise "the world" over whom the Evil One has control. Those who have overcome "the world" through Christ are no longer under Satan's control. At the

---

375. 1 John 3:11-15
376. John 8:44
377. 1 John 2:13-14
378. 1 John 5:19

point when they declare their allegiance to the Lord, the children of God are still very much *in the world* but no longer *of the world*.[379]

In his Apocalypse, John takes note that Satan (that old serpent, the devil) leads the whole world astray.[380] After what he did in the Garden, can there be any doubt about what a huge impact the Evil One has had in introducing sin to humankind? Little wonder that Jesus referred to him as the prince of this world.[381]

But don't attach more to that designation than is warranted. Having gotten the ball of evil rolling, the Evil One is rightly associated with a world now permeated with sin. Yet if the Evil One were suddenly to disappear, the world he tainted would still exist. The world of immoral people.[382] The world in whose ways you yourself once lived.[383] The world whose pattern you must not be conformed to.[384] The world whose basic principles once enslaved you.[385] The world you have overcome victoriously by faith in Christ.[386] The world to which you no longer belong.[387] The world you must never again love.[388]

Some might call it a distinction without a difference, but your day-to-day battle is not directly with the Evil One, any more than Allied soldiers fighting against the Nazi regime did hand-to-hand combat with Hitler himself. Your daily battle is

---

379. John 15:19; 17:15-16; 1 Corinthians 5:9-10
380. Revelation 12:9
381. John 12:31; 14:30
382. Luke 16:8; 1 Corinthians 5:9-10
383. Ephesians 2:1-2
384. Romans 12:2
385. Galatians 4:3; Colossians 2:20-22
386. 1 John 5:4-5
387. John 15:19; 17:14
388. 1 John 2:15

with the diabolical regime of sin the Evil One instigated, for everything that is sinful comes from "the world" he initiated — whether the lust of the eyes or any other sinful craving.[389]

The distinction between Satan's personal intervention in your life and his figurehead role as the originator of all temptation is important in that it helps put the focus on what *you* personally control rather than on what *Satan* personally controls. While the Evil One is responsible for the world of sin, you yourself have control over whether his sin system will control you! As you think about the sin in your life, are you in control, or out of control?

The temptation conundrum...

*A*re you suggesting that Satan's power has been curtailed? Actually, yes. Do you remember when in the week prior to his crucifixion Jesus told the crowds that the time for judgment of the world had come (not meaning the final Judgment)?[390] "The time has come," he said, "for the prince of this world to be driven out." When was that to be? "When I'm lifted up," Jesus said, referring to his death on the cross.

In his final discourse to the Eleven (Judas having already left to carry out his dastardly betrayal), Jesus had a tone of immediacy in his voice when he said to them, "I won't be speaking with you much longer, because the prince of this world is coming. The Evil One has no hold over me, but he must be allowed his day so that the world can see that I am obedient to my Father."[391]

---

389. 1 John 2:16
390. John 12:31-33
391. John 14:30-31

With the same urgency, Jesus said to them, "The prince of this world stands condemned even now."[392] Since the Evil One had been under condemnation from the time of the Great Uprising, you can appreciate that Jesus had a more immediate condemnation in mind, one to take place within hours.

By orchestrating Jesus' death on the cross, that ancient serpent would "bruise the heel" of Eve's offspring. But in that same dark hour the Evil One would have his own head crushed by the Son.[393] No longer would the Evil One have mastery over death. Dying on the cross, Jesus destroyed the power of him who had brought death to humankind. In doing so, Jesus took away any need for man to fear any finality in death.[394]

As is evident, the cross was not the first defeat of the Evil One. The first defeat, of course, was in the Great Uprising. The second defeat came at the Evil One's failed attempted to kill the newborn Christ, using Herod as his hit man.[395] Then came the Evil One's humiliation in the desert of temptation when he unsuccessfully attempted to bring Jesus down. Jesus' victory in that one-on-one confrontation had the effect of "tying up the strong man," as it were, enabling Jesus to drive out the Evil One's demons from those who were diabolically possessed.[396]

Yet it was on the cross that Jesus finally and fully overpowered the Evil One, together with the horrendous sin and spiritual death Satan had brought to the earth. By nailing sin and death to the cross, Jesus made a public spectacle of the Evil One and all he represented, thereby triumphing over any authority the Evil One

---

392. John 16:11
393. Genesis 3:15
394. Hebrews 2:14-15
395. Matthew 2:13, 19; Cf. Revelation 2:4b-5
396. Matthew 12:29; Mark 3:27; Luke 11:21-22

might have claimed.[397] From the cross and resurrection onward, the Evil One was a "dead man walking," as you sometimes say of death-row inmates. Not yet destroyed, but condemned!

Jesus also triumphed over those Jews and Romans who acted as surrogates for the Evil One in ordering and executing Jesus' death. Had any of them fully understood the cosmic significance of what they were doing, they wouldn't have laid a finger on the Son.[398] Indeed, had the Evil One himself calculated more carefully the implications of Jesus' death (which canceled the penalty of man's sin), he would have done everything in his power to keep Jesus *off* the cross! In his rush to win the battle, the Evil One lost the war and thereby forever lost his dominion over humankind.

_ 12 ´

*I*f Satan was defeated at the cross, why is he still a **force to be reckoned with?** Because his spirit is still very much alive and well in the system of sin he foisted on the world, and certainly in those who are disobedient.[399] When I say *spirit*, I'm not speaking of "evil spirit," in the same sense as demons (or indeed Satan himself who is a spirit being!), but, as it were, in the "spirit of the age," or the "spirit of fair play," or the "spirit of giving." The evil ways of the world that linger to this day reflect the spirit of the Evil One who rules over his airy kingdom of rebel angels.

You get a sense of this "spirit" when Paul references the Evil One without intending to say he is the actual culprit. Remember when Paul told the Corinthians how he feared that "just as Eve was deceived by the serpent's cunning," they too might be

---

397. Colossians 2:13-15
398. Luke 23:34; 1 Corinthians 2:6-8
399. Ephesians 2:1-2

led astray from their devotion to Christ?[400] In Corinth, the spirit of deception was alive and well, just as when it was manifest in the serpent.

Because the Evil One is the initiating source of all evil, his lasting spirit colors every act that ends up being sin. In what you call the "Sermon on the Mount," Jesus railed against those who are constantly saying, "I swear" as if somehow that vow were necessary for anyone to believe them or to trust their promises. Instead, Jesus called for people simply to let their "Yes" really mean "Yes," and their "No" really mean "No"![401] The practice of constantly invoking God's name in the form of an oath (particularly when you don't mean what you say) comes from the Evil One, said Jesus. Satan doesn't literally put the oath in one's mouth, but anyone who speaks untruthfully is mimicking the falsehood so characteristic of the Evil One. His spirit is their spirit.

The Evil One's pervasive spirit is so enduring that Peter specifically invokes the devil's name when warning Christ's followers to be alert and self-controlled. "Your enemy the devil," says Peter, "prowls around like a roaring lion looking for someone to devour."[402] If that sounds like the Evil One is on the loose, he's not. One thing's for sure: the Evil One is not omnipresent as is the Holy One, so he couldn't possibly be tempting every human being at every moment of every day even if he wanted to. But his spirit is so pervasive that it's in every nook and cranny of your world—deceiving, seducing, and causing destruction.

If I didn't fear your carrying the analogy too far, I'd suggest that the trail of slime left by the Evil One is a kind of devilish

---

400. 2 Corinthians 11:3-4
401. Matthew 5:33-37
402. 1 Peter 5:8-9

Speaking of the Devil

"deism" in which the Evil One wound up the clock of sin and walked away, leaving it ticking on nicely till the end of time. Only it wasn't his choice to "walk away," and his departure certainly wasn't out of a sense of indifference. Of this you can be sure: the Evil One is keenly proud of how well his "clock" (how do you say it?) takes a lickin' but keeps on tickin'!

So when Peter says, "Resist him," what he really means is: Resist all that the Evil One stands for. If you think that particular spin does violence to what Peter seems to be plainly saying (and I can see why you would think so), consider carefully the dynamics that would have to be in play were it truly a one-to-one confrontation between you and the devil.

For starters, you'd have to know specifically that you were under personal threat from the Evil One—just as Jesus knew in the desert. Since you can never know that for certain, you must fall back on doing exactly what Peter went on to explain. At all times, you must stand firm in the faith *as if* you were doing actual battle moment by moment with the Evil One. Whether or not the Evil One is actually ever in your face, you must live your life with that presumption in mind.

Are you experiencing suffering as are many of your brothers and sisters in Christ around the world? Then you are under threat! Are you anxious in any way? Then you are under threat! Do you chafe at those in authority over you? Then you are under threat! Because of the oppressiveness of an evil world, not a day goes by that you're not under threat. It's not literally true that the Evil One is out there peeping in your window waiting for just the right opening, but you should always keep in mind Peter's graphic picture of the Evil One as a stalking lion. To resist *sin* is to resist *him*. Resist *him*, and *sin* will flee from you as surely as the Evil One himself.

And how are you to resist the devil? By submitting your life wholly to God. Come near to God, and he will come near to you.[403] As long as you are standing with the Holy One, you have nothing to fear from the devil's perverse plan for your life.

*a*re you saying that Satan doesn't tempt us? At least not in the way that you might imagine. Yes, I know what Paul said to the Corinthians about the Evil One tempting husbands and wives who unwisely allow their sexual relationship (or lack of it) to put them at risk.[404] Because of Satan's role in the first temptation, and in the temptation of Jesus, the Evil One is the compelling, quintessential caricature of *all* temptation. Yet if Paul had left Satan completely out of the picture, husbands and wives would still need to be on guard in maintaining sexual purity "because there is so much immorality," as some translations put it. I suppose I'm not the best one to say so, but it seems there's wisdom in Paul's advice.

As Paul says later in the same letter, temptation is common to man.[405] That's not because the Evil One is personally sitting on each and every person's shoulder, whispering seductive lines in their ear. Given the fact that right choices are always paired with wrong choices, temptation is virtually built into human choice. Which is the first reason why with every temptation there is always a way of escape. With every choice, you can choose rightly or wrongly. Neither God nor the Evil One forces your choice.

For Christ's faithful disciples, there is a more important reason why there's always a way of escape. Simply put, God provides

---

403. James 4:7-8
404. 1 Corinthians 7:2-5
405. 1 Corinthians 10:13

it! But be careful here. He'll never shove you involuntarily down that path to safety. You yourself must see the opening and take it. When you yield to temptation, as you often do, it's not because there is no good escape exit. All the exits are clearly marked! As I suspect you're all too aware, the problem is never the *way*, but the *will*.

Have you ever been curious as to why James (who urges resisting the devil) never mentions the Evil One when he writes specifically and directly about temptation? Ruling out any chance that God is the source of temptation, James says that you are tempted when you are dragged away and enticed by your own desires, a process which eventually results in sin and death.[406] It's kind of like the dog that didn't bark in that story told by one of your mystery writers. At first, the detective (Holmes, was it?) is stumped as to "who dunnit." Suddenly it dawns on him that the dog didn't bark, which turns out to be a crucial fact pointing to the killer. In this case, James' failure to mention the Evil One points the finger of suspicion *away from* Satan.

There's another crucial passage where the dog doesn't bark. It's that classic passage of self-flagellation where Paul bemoans not doing what he knows he should, and doing precisely what he knows he shouldn't.[407] In the final analysis, Paul resorts to hyperbole, lamenting that sin must be living in him (as if some autonomous drone!), but — crucially — there's not the first mention of the Evil One.

And in the gloomy quiet of Gethsemane, not a distant dog is heard to bark when Jesus says to his sleepy disciples, "Watch and pray, so that you not fall into temptation."[408] Wouldn't

---

406. James 1:13-15
407. Romans 7:14-20
408. Matthew 26:40-41; Mark 14:37-38; Luke 22:45-46

that have been the perfect time to mention that the Evil One was lurking in the shadows? That, at any moment, fiery darts of the devil would turn that peaceful garden into Armageddon? Or that if the ancient serpent could so easily seduce Eve in the Garden, he could just as easily seduce them in the olive garden where they lay asleep? But no dog barks when you'd most expect it. In the midst of the highest Satanic alert since the Great Uprising, Jesus said not a word about the Evil One! I should know. I was there....[409]

Here's something to ponder: Suppose you knew for a fact that Satan personally had nothing whatsoever to do with tempting you to sin. Do you think you'd be free of all temptation?

*H*ow are we supposed to understand "the Lord's prayer"? I take it you mean the parts about temptation and being delivered from evil?[410] I can see where this could be perplexing. When you pray that your heavenly Father not lead you into temptation, you're obviously aware that God isn't in the business of tempting folks.[411] Your prayer, then, is that God will actively lead you *away* from temptation—particularly away from anything that might sorely test your faith. "Give me wisdom and resolve to overcome temptation," might better capture the idea.

I suspect I already know your next question about this model prayer, as it always seems to be a favorite query. Everybody wants to know whether they are to pray for deliverance from *evil* generally or from *the Evil One* specifically. Actually, this

---

409. Luke 22:43
410. Matthew 6:13
411. James 1:13

question is a microcosm of the whole conversation about the nature of evil and the Evil One.

For anyone not yet in the know, the original word in your text can be translated either way, though it does have the definite article, suggesting *the* evil, as in the Evil One. But it's not really a matter of translation once you understand the inextricable connection between evil and the Evil One. To say the one is to say the other. *The Evil One* is but the personification of *evil*; and *evil* is but the natural extension of him who is the *Evil One*.

The only real difference is the degree to which Satan is seen to be involved actively in the process of temptation. As we've already discussed, it's not his personal involvement you need worry about. What you must be aware of and resist to the utmost is his value system. His character. His agenda. His own sin as it represents yours; and your own sin as it reflects his.

By contrast, Jesus wasn't thinking about sin in some general sense when he prayed to his Father to protect the Eleven from the Evil One.[412] Jesus was keenly aware of how seriously his chosen apostles would come under withering enemy fire during their ministry. *Evil* would always be their enemy, but *the Evil One* himself had each of them personally in his sights. With one of the apostles having already become Satan's victim, Jesus was putting a divine hedge around those who remained.

Your own prayers are somewhat different. If you yourself are "delivered from evil," you are delivered from the Evil One. If you are "delivered from the Evil One," you are delivered from evil. So pray however you please. Just pray!

---

412. John 17:15

Angels, Demons, and the Devil

About John's Apocalypse...

[handwritten: Lesson #5]

What are we meant to understand about Satan from Revelation? Jesus' revelation to John was intended first and foremost to reassure first-century believers facing severe persecution that, in the end, God wins and the Evil One loses. Which meant that they too would win, that steadfastness in the face of martyrdom would be well worth whatever cost it might entail, and that any loss on this side would be more than adequately compensated for on the other side. In the midst of persecution, what they needed to focus on boiled down to two things: purity and faithfulness.

At the heart of John's Apocalypse you can see a graphic depiction of cataclysmic events leading to periods of persecution and the victory of those who persevere.[413] As always, the Evil One plays a starring role in the epic, being the one who instigates the persecution and wars against the faithful. As "the dragon," Satan conspires with "the two beasts" (one coming out of the sea, the other emerging from the earth)[414] and with "the false prophet"[415] against the forces of good. In the end, predictably, the Evil One and his co-conspirators are overwhelmed and defeated.

What you see throughout John's spectacular vision is familiar territory, as if a recapitulation of the whole of Scripture from Creation to consummation. For example, there is language reprising the Great Uprising, complete with a celestial battle and the casting down to earth of the Evil One and his angels.

---

413. Revelation 12:1-17
414. Revelation 13:1-18
415. Revelation 16:13; 19:20; 20:10

There are also vivid images of a pregnant woman (invoking fascinating overtones of both Eve and Mary). Despite every temptation to spin John's vision in other directions, the picture being painted is that of the church in the midst of persecution at a time when it is about to be given birth into an explosive period of growth and expansion (represented by the male child, with intriguing allusions to Jesus himself).

Yet the heroes of the piece are neither the pregnant woman, nor the dragon (representing the Evil One), nor Christ himself, but Christian martyrs who remain faithful even under the threat of death. In the face of every assault that the Evil One can hurl, the faithful overcome him by the blood of the Lamb—in the same way that Jesus himself overcame the Evil One when he spilled that very blood on the cross. And here's what I love most. When the Evil One sees that he is as defeated by the martyrs as he was by Christ, he skulks away, knowing that his time is short! Makes you want to stand up and cheer, doesn't it!

The rest of what you read in John's Apocalypse regarding the Evil One is something we've already mentioned or likely will touch on in our discussion about demons. But there is one thing we haven't talked about. I wonder if you've ever thought of the irony of the two "trinities"? Just as the Holy One appears as Father, Son, and Holy Spirit, Jesus himself twice refers to the Evil One as serpent, devil, and Satan.[416] Laying those two "trinities" side by side, it's intriguing that the closest the Evil One ever came to being incarnate (as was the *Son*) was as a serpent! Pretty much says it all, doesn't it?

This ironic parallel brings to mind something we angels have observed with much curiosity. Have you ever considered

---

416. Revelation 12:9; 20:2

whether humans might have invested too much in the word *trinity*, suggesting as it does a kind of celestial triumvirate comprised of three separate and distinct divinities? (Praise God that the Evil One is certainly not three distinct individuals!)

As long as you are on this side and not the other, I wouldn't expect you to appreciate fully the mysterious dynamics that make it possible for the *One God* to be Father, Son, and Holy Spirit.[417] I would simply caution against speaking so glibly about the Holy One's triune nature that some people get the wrong idea altogether. From my unique vantage point, I have seen every aspect of the Holy One, including his presence on both sides of the Great Divide. Even for us angels, what is mystery for you is altogether wondrous!

Lesson 9

Why does Satan figure so prominently in the seven letters? As your question indicates, the Evil One gets dishonorable mention all throughout the letters to the seven churches in Asia. Whatever particular problem is being addressed in any one of the churches, the Evil One seems to get all the blame!

The two curious references to the "synagogue of Satan," for example, tie in naturally with the Apocalypse's overall theme of persecution.[418] The phrase itself is yet one more example of how Satan's name is often used as a kind of short-hand for evil, not meant to be taken literally. Why attach the Evil One's name to a synagogue? Because, in claiming to be faithful, God-fearing Jews when they are not, these folks are liars—just like their father the devil. They are also slanderous, as is the Evil

---

417. Deuteronomy 6:4
418. Revelation 2:9; 3:9

One. Most of all, they are attempting to destroy the children of God, something the Evil One would do himself if he could. Which explains why Jesus says to John that "the devil" will put some of the disciples in prison to test them.[419]

Don't get thrown off by the word *synagogue*. As is obvious from the fact that the word is used in letters to two different churches (Smyrna and Philadelphia), no formal, official synagogue is being referenced. Rather, the term is descriptive of those who assemble as Jews but, by their attitudes and actions, give more honor to the Evil One than to God.

Continuing to associate the Evil One with various challenging situations being addressed, Jesus acknowledges that the saints in Pergamum live where Satan lives and "has his throne" (metaphorically speaking).[420] That's some indictment against Pergamum! Truth be known, the same could have been said of many ancient cities, and — as you are well aware — could apply with equal force far and wide today.

To the church in Thyatira Jesus speaks figuratively of "the woman Jezebel," a false prophetess who is misleading the disciples into idolatry and sexual immorality by convincing them of certain "deep spiritual secrets."[421] They're deep alright! Like a pile of manure! Fitting, I'd say, for the Lord of the flies with whom Jesus associates this seductive pack of lies.

In case you wonder whether throughout our conversation I've perhaps overstated the case for the Evil One often being spoken of merely figuratively as an icon for evil, I draw your

---

419. Revelation 2:10
420. Revelation 2:13
421. Revelation 2:20-25

attention here to the woman Jesus calls "Jezebel." It's the same idea really. Like characterizing someone as a Judas or a Hitler, you need only say the word *Jezebel* and everyone knows you're talking about an ambitious, manipulative, wicked woman. (Interesting, isn't it, how two different icons are so much alike that one could be the very icon of the other!)

*W*hat does Revelation tell us about Satan's ultimate end? You don't need me to tell you that! The imagery is all there, of judgment, torment, and final defeat in that apocalyptic "lake of fire."[422] Don't forget, it's Jesus' own words, precisely reiterating what he had said during his ministry about the great Day of Judgment and the dire fate awaiting those unrighteous "goats" on his left. Their sentence? Being cast into the same apocalyptic fire prepared for the Evil One and his angels.[423]

If the Evil One is ever released from prison and "given his day to deceive the nations," never fear. Any fleeting victories he may have will pale in comparison to his own ultimate and final defeat.

Yet don't focus on the Evil One, except as a picture of all those who rebel against the Holy One. *His* fate is *their* fate. *His* end is *their* end. *His* eternal destruction is *theirs*. If you understand nothing else at all about John's Revelation, understand that!

But not just that. Understand also the abiding victory of those who maintain moral purity in a licentious world and remain faithful to God no matter what trials, persecutions, or opposition comes their way. *Your* way....

---

422. Revelation 20:10
423. Matthew 25:31-46

The really BIG questions...

Why would God permit Satan to exist and spread his evil? It's the classic question isn't it? And you are certainly not the first to ask. In fact, the prophet Habbakuk dared to pose virtually that same question directly to God, complete with a compelling argument as to why the Holy One should *not* permit evil in the world. "Your eyes are too pure to look on evil," the prophet reasoned. "Surely you can't tolerate wrong! So why do you permit the treacherous to exist?"[424]

I have to say that I myself have had reservations about God's judgment in this regard. Not that I question his sovereign right to do as he pleases, only that the problem of evil (and the Evil One in particular) is not an easy question for either angel or man. But let me share some of the thoughts that give me a peace about all this at least for myself.

Let me say first of all that, as an angel, what amazes me almost as much as permitting the Evil One to have power and persuasion over man is permitting Habbakuk's frank question itself to find a place in the revealed Word! Know any other sovereign who would allow to be recorded an accusing demand that he justify his actions to his subjects? Speaks volumes about God's character, suggesting that—whatever reasons he may have—they are *benevolent* reasons.

Then, of course, there is the obvious fact that the Holy One also permits man to be manipulated, seduced, harassed, and oppressed by fellow human beings who are evil. It may beg the

---

424. Habakkuk 1:13

original question, but if this is the case, it's not such a great stretch for God to have permitted a kind of "super-evil personality" to do the same. Think of it as Hitler by a factor of millions.

Which leads to consideration of the options originally available to God. Naturally, one option was for the sovereign Creator of the universe himself to introduce evil directly into his creation and specifically commission the Evil One as his agent—all to his own glory. Nothing intrinsically would prevent the Lord of the Universe from doing that...other than his innate character as the Holy One. In his pristine holiness, it is not possible that God could be the author of evil or appoint Satan as his alter ego to tempt man when he has ruled himself out of doing such a thing personally.[425]

And here's where the options get tight. To forbid evil outright, and (by extension) evil's instruments whether celestial or human, it would have been necessary for the Holy One to deny freedom of will to his creatures. To take away *their* options. Yet, it's clear that the Holy One chose freedom over manipulation for his subjects. The risk that all of us (angels and humans alike) might use our freedom to choose evil rather than good was a risk that the Holy One was willing to accept in exchange for knowing that, if men and angels freely chose to serve and obey him, it would be *genuine* rather than contrived by sovereign determination. I don't think I ever really appreciated what a great risk the Holy One took until I heard the first rumblings of the Great Uprising. Nor did I fully appreciate what a great God the Holy One is until I saw for myself how real the risk was from the very beginning.

---

425. James 1:13

Speaking of the Devil

Still, I agree with you that the Holy One could easily have banished the Evil One completely out of existence from the first moment of the Rebellion. Or permanently quarantined him and his nefarious demons so that man would not be swayed by their influence or ever physically possessed. This, I believe, is the trickier question. Did man *need* a tempter? Perhaps not, but apparently the Holy One believed man needed a *reminder*. Something tangible to dissuade one from evil. Add to that a period of heightened spiritual warfare during Christ's ministry and the ministry of his apostles, not simply to confirm Jesus' lordship, but to highlight the seriousness of the battle between good and evil.

When all is said and done, the Evil One is God's ultimate parable showing the heinousness of evil and its destructive end. What is it you say about a picture being worth a thousand words...?

So doesn't that make Satan God's servant? Not a chance! Take away the "picture worth a thousand words," and man would still have every reason to choose good and shun evil. Don't forget that under the old covenant the people of Israel had only the slightest inkling of the Evil One and his rebel angels. Yet they were expected to take evil seriously, even without any caricature of a red-suited devil or a more theologically-sophisticated Satan figure.

Don't forget, too, that the Evil One didn't *have to be* the Evil One. He certainly wasn't created evil, and you can be sure that the Holy One did not purposely transform him into the evil being Satan became by his own choice. So it's a matter of God taking Satan's perverted free will and employing it in alignment with his own divine will. What Satan intends for evil, God permits for a higher good.

Incidentally, don't confuse foreknowledge and foreordination. To *know* in advance is not to *ordain* in advance. (When you watch an instant replay, does the fact that you know in advance what you're about to see mean that it *had to happen* that way in real time?)

The only way in which the Evil One even remotely can be said to be God's servant is as the wicked nations of Assyria and Babylon (both evil to the core) were used by God to upbraid rebellious Israel. God took evil nations that were already intent on destroying Israel and used that evil to chastise his people before turning the tables and destroying those very same evil nations.

But it goes too far to suggest that God purposely dispatched the Evil One to do his bidding—as if Satan was God's servant to inflict Paul's "thorn in the flesh."[426] (Paul is speaking metaphorically.) Or that Satan acted as God's servant inflicting pain on Job so that the story of Job's steadfastness could be told. (Remember, it's an historically-inspired *story*.) Nor certainly that the Holy One specially commissioned the Evil One as his servant to make sure the Son was crucified on the cross! If what the Evil One does on his own initiative sometimes turns out to serve God's purposes, it doesn't make him God's servant. God forbid!

If there is a real sense in which the Evil One represents the evil in your own life, you must be careful what you think and say about him. For if Satan is *God's* servant simply because his evil sometimes plays into God's hands, does that make you *Satan's* servant simply because your evil sometimes plays into Satan's hands? Actually, that's a trick question, the answer being yet another of those pesky "yes-and-no" answers. To the extent that you do evil, then, yes, you *are* serving the Evil One. Yet, as

---

426. 2 Corinthians 12:7-10

a committed disciple of Christ (if you are one), you are a servant of God, not Satan.

All the more reason, then, to take a long, hard look at your life and ask the daunting question: Are you a servant of God, yet acting like a servant of Satan?

Angels, Demons, and the Devil

Part Three

Speaking of Demons

Jesus' mission can be described as being twofold:
it is a battle against the demons, and it is a battle for men.

— Helmut Thielicke

You seem to have a particular interest in demons — who they are, how they operate, whether they are still a force to be reckoned with, and so forth. There's much to say about the demons, and sadly much that has been said about them without careful study or reflection. Indeed, much of it is sheer foolishness. So I welcome the opportunity to share with you whatever I can. As always, there are some aspects of our discussion which are either limited by divine directive or clouded by the usual limitations of human understanding. But if you're happy with those parameters, we can give it a go.

*a*re "demons" simply shorthand for disease and mental illness? Definitely not! Demons, I assure you, are real. Demons have personalities.[427] Demons move from one victim to another.[428] Demons *talk*![429] What disease do you know of that can do that?

If you look carefully at the Gospel accounts, you will see any number of times when demon-possession is listed separately from the miraculous healing of diseases. Merely consider Mark's report that "Jesus healed many from their various diseases. He also drove out many demons...."[430] Mark was right to make that crisp distinction. So was Matthew when he described the crowds who flocked to Jesus bringing those who were ill with diseases, suffering severe pain, and having seizures, or were paralyzed *or demon-possessed*.[431] And Luke makes the same distinction.[432]

Remember when Jesus sent word to Herod that he was too busy driving out demons and healing people to worry about any threats from "that fox?"[433] Jesus was talking about two distinct aspects of his many miracles. And when Jesus commissioned his apostles for both phases of their ministry (both before and after his ascension), he gave them authority to drive out evil spirits *and* to heal every disease and sickness. He told them specifically to heal the sick, cleanse the lepers, raise the dead, *and* drive out demons.[434]

---

427. Luke 8:30-31
428. Matthew 8:28-32; Luke 8:33
429. Mark 1:23-26
430. Mark 1:34
431. Matthew 4:23-24
432. Luke 7:21; Acts 5:16; 8:7
433. Luke 13:31-32
434. Matthew 10:1, 8; Mark 6:7, 13; 16:17

But I appreciate why people might be confused about this since there are numerous passages where specific illnesses are directly attributed to demon-possession. There's that demon-possessed man, for example, who was blind and mute.[435] And the man whose son was deaf, mute, and suffering from seizures.[436] And the one who could not talk until the evil spirit was driven out of him.[437] And, of course, there's that mentally disturbed Gerasene who practiced self-mutilation.[438]

Speaking more generally, Peter told Cornelius the Roman centurion that Jesus had "healed" all who were under the power of the devil.[439] I'm also reminded of that extraordinary miracle God worked through Paul wherein even handkerchiefs and aprons that touched him were taken to those who were sick. As if hand in glove, their evil spirits left them and their illnesses were cured.[440]

The fact is that demons sometimes caused physical and mental trauma in the lives of their victims, such that driving out the demons resulted in healing the particular disease or mental state being manifest. But it was not invariably the case that demon-possession was to be equated with illness. The last thing you want to assume is that "demon" was a metaphor for disease or insanity, or that this was simply the way people described illnesses before there was more sophisticated knowledge about medical conditions.

Even in today's more sophisticated medical age, you still hear folks talking nonsense about "demon drink" or someone

---

435. Matthew 12:22
436. Matthew 17:14-15; Mark 9:17-25
437. Matthew 9:32-33
438. Mark 5:2-5
439. Acts 10:37-38
440. Acts 19:11-12

"chasing his demons." (There's even that interesting play on words between intoxicating liquor and "spirits.") But such expressions are only that: *expressions*. There is no substance or reality behind those statements, and certainly no *real* demons. When metaphors turn into myths, they become demon metaphors!

*W*hat is the difference between a demon and an unclean spirit? Nothing at all. In fact, an "unclean spirit" is just another way of expressing "evil spirit" — both of which refer to demons, which themselves are fallen angels. Sometimes I hear humans talking about "unclean spirits" or "evil spirits" as if there were various species of spiritual entities distinct from Satan's rebel angels. But I assure you there are no evil gremlins or ghosts out there, either on earth or floating around in the heavenlies.

When you read the Gospels, you can sometimes see one of the writers referring to evil or unclean spirits, then speaking of demons in the very next breath. Mark does that in the first chapter of his Gospel account.[441] In the opening text, Mark records Jesus entering the synagogue at Capernaum and driving out an "evil spirit" whom Jesus rebuked for calling him the Holy One of God. Then, only a few verses later, Mark speaks more generally about Jesus driving out many "demons" — not letting them speak because they knew who he was. In both references, Mark obviously has in mind the same evil creatures.

In his parallel account, Luke first records Jesus driving out the "evil spirit" in the synagogue, then immediately refers back to

---

441. Mark 1:23-28, 32-34

that same "evil spirit" as "the demon."[442] As you can appreciate, the term of choice for first-century Jews was *evil spirit* or *unclean spirit*, which explains its more frequent usage in instances of specific demon-possession.

Not to be confused with any of the above is Zechariah's prophecy of a coming time when idols, deceiving prophets, and "the unclean spirit" would be removed from the land.[443] Zechariah is not referring to one or more demons here, but (as other versions point out more clearly) to "the spirit of impurity" hanging like a thick fog over the land. That "spirit of impurity" was caused by the people's craving for idolatry and willingness to accept the teaching of false prophets. Nothing to do with evil (or unclean) spirits.

*W*hat is the connection between demons and goats? So you've heard, have you! It's mostly a matter of terminology, really. One of the words often translated as "demon" is closely associated with goats. (Calling them "satyrs," reflecting Greek mythology, is a stretch.) These goats (a.k.a. "demons") usually inhabited arid places, like spooky deserts, especially at night. So you could also speak of them as "night creatures." Given the popular image of spooky creatures haunting dark, deserted places, you can see how some folks would instantly think of "demons." Naturally, goats would be a far more tenuous connection, but make no mistake in that regard. Goats aren't demons, and demons aren't goats.

At least not *real* goats. One of the complicating factors in your trying to understand demons is that "goat worship" was practiced in a number of ancient cultures and was a recurring

---

442. Luke 4:33-37
443. Zechariah 13:2

problem in Israel as well. That's why the laws of Moses explicitly prohibited goat worship.[444] (Incidentally, it wasn't *devil worship* being prohibited, as your King James Version would tell you. The king's translators went a bit over the top in their use of the word *devil* where either *demon* or, as here, *goat* would give you a clearer picture.)

Do you remember how Jeroboam installed his own priests (in lieu of the Levites) to oversee the idolatry he established in his high places? Some of the idols he set up were goat idols, like those the Israelites had seen down in Egypt.[445]

Once you see the ties between goats and *idolatry* and goats and *demons*, you can better appreciate the further connection between *demons* and *idolatry*. When the ancients spoke of "demon worship," they typically associated it with idolatry, plain and simple, whether the particular idol was a goat, a calf, or even the likeness of man. In ancient times, *demons* most often meant nothing more than *gods*. False, non-existent gods, to be sure, but behind whatever rock or stone or graven image was being worshiped was usually a hovering spiritual deity or force which the idol was thought to represent. Those "spirits" in the people's imagined spirit-world were their revered "demons" — sometimes malevolent, but more often viewed as benevolent. So the demons of the ancient world (as even recognized by John's Apocalypse[446]) were not necessarily *evil spirits*, as one might think of demons, but merely *gods* of all sorts in the panoply of idolatry.

In case you've ever wondered, this explains what the apostle Paul was talking about in his first letter to the saints at Corinth

---

444. Leviticus 17:7
445. 2 Chronicles 11:15
446. Revelation 9:20

when he said, first of all, that so-called "gods" represented by idols are nothing at all; that there is but one God, the Father, and only one Lord, Jesus Christ.[447] And that, therefore, the pagan sacrifices offered to "demons" (which is to say false, imaginary gods), are in opposition to the one true God. How then, Paul asks, can any believer drink the cup of the Lord (which puts one in communion with God) yet also drink "the cup of demons" (which fosters a meaningless relationship with God-denying idolatry)?[448]

For believers in Christ to participate in idolatry would be to repeat the mistake of the Israelites when they turned to the false gods of their heathen neighbors. They had sacrificed to "demons" — which were not God.[449] Quite incredibly, they had even sacrificed their children to "demons" — which is to say the Canaanite deities, not the demons who are evil spirits from the celestial realm.[450]

When God was instructing Moses concerning the coming Passover, he said that he would be passing through Egypt, striking down every firstborn and bringing judgment on all of Egypt's "gods." Read *demons*.[451] When David contrasts his praise for the Creator of the heavens to the idol "gods" of the nations, again read *demons*.[452] And when Isaiah pronounces God's judgment against Egypt for consulting their "idols," one could just as easily insert the word *demons*. In the Old Testament, "demons" had little or nothing to do with evil celestial beings. Typically, the term *demon* referred to idols, idolatry, and pagan gods. Or goats!

---

447. 1 Corinthians 8:4-6
448. 1 Corinthians 10:14-22
449. Deuteronomy 32:17
450. Psalm 106:37-38
451. Exodus 12:12
452. 1 Chronicles 16:26; Psalm 96:5

Which brings us full-circle to God's punishment of all this idolatrous "demon worship." Ironically, when Isaiah spoke of idolatrous Babylon's ultimate devastation, he suggests that the land would be laid so bare that only desert creatures, jackals, owls, and "wild goats" could exist where humans once had lived. And the same is true when Isaiah spoke of Edom's destruction—that it would be fit only for desert animals, night creatures, and "wild goats."[453] Call them "demons," if you wish. John certainly did in his Apocalypse when describing the fall of yet another Babylon (Babylon the Great).[454] But rather than being a bunch of "demon goats," John's demons were "unclean spirits." Those evil spirits are much closer to the kind of demons I suspect you're most interested in. Am I right?

*a***re you saying that the Jews didn't believe in evil spirits?** Far from it. Borrowing from their pagan neighbors, the Israelites were increasingly attracted to gods, demigods, and other-worldly spirits. While in Babylonian captivity, especially, the Jews became enchanted with Chaldean and Persian belief in both good and evil spirits. A certain dualism was accepted in which there were good spirits calling one to right conduct and evil spirits tempting one toward sin.

By the time of Christ, the Jews had a fairly complex belief system including angels and demons (all, that is, except the Sadducees, who did not believe in either angels or spirits—whether evil spirits or benevolent spirits).[455] There were even stories circulating about the origin of demons. The Book of Enoch, as I noted earlier, first gave rise to the popular rumor

---

453. Isaiah 13:21; 34:14
454. Revelation 18:2
455. Acts 23:8-9

about evil spirits being the offspring of rogue angels who intermarried with humans. Still others believed them to be superhuman ghosts of the dead who roamed about as specters and vampires.

In the first century, rabbinic practices of dealing with perceived "demons" mirrored contemporary pagan remedies, including the use of foul-smelling odors, nasty-tasting potions, and physical torture. Scary "demons" could also be kept at bay with phylacteries, amulets, ablutions, and arcane rituals. Not surprisingly, the sanctimonious Pharisees believed that the best way to ward off demons was found in strict law-keeping!

It is well known, of course, that "demon-possession" was taken for granted by first-century Jews, who attributed all sorts of maladies and conditions to these variously-defined "demons." In fact, by the time of Christ, the Jews had a long-established tradition of "demon exorcism" (at least, what was *thought* to be exorcism of what were *believed* to be demons). Jewish exorcism was as much a fraud as Jewish sorcery, based as it was on intricately prescribed formulas, incantations, and mystical words thought to have magical powers.

When the seven sons of Sceva (a chief priest in Ephesus) observed Paul expelling genuine demons in the name of the Lord Jesus, they concluded that appealing to the "Lord Jesus" must be especially magical, so they started invoking Jesus' name as part of their exorcisms. But their "magic" suddenly backfired when a real, live demon beat them up and sent them packing, naked and wounded! What the evil spirit most exposed, however, was the fraudulent exorcisms they practiced. "I know Jesus, and I know of Paul," said the demon, "but who are *you*!"[456]

---

456. Acts 19:11-16

It's no wonder that Jesus was particularly scornful of any so-called "miracle workers" who would simulate miraculous healings and exorcisms in the name of Christ. Looking ahead to the Day of Judgment, Jesus said there will be plenty of religious folks who will plead (even sincerely), "Didn't we prophesy, and do miracles, and drive out demons—all in your name?" They are as self-deluded as their captivated audiences are deceived! In a twist on what the demon said about not knowing the sons of Sceva, Jesus himself will say to these imposters, "I never knew you. Get away from me!"[457]

By contrast, there was the sincere follower of Christ who really and truly did cast out demons in the name of Jesus. Although he was not one of the apostles, he was acting in good faith and was defended by the Lord when the apostles got huffy and warned him off.[458] In this unique case, Jesus wasn't authorizing or encouraging all of his disciples to drive out demons, but used this incident to rebuke the Twelve for taking it upon themselves to decide who was acting on behalf of the kingdom and who was not.

The Pharisees were just as "territorial" as the apostles. You may recall the occasion when Jesus was accused by the Pharisees of driving out demons by the power of Beelzebub.[459] In response, Jesus asked them by what power their own exorcists drove out demons—not meaning that they actually did, but that the Pharisees approved of such fraudulent chicanery while condemning Jesus for driving out real demons.

In addition to having an eclectic theology of make-believe "demons" that could accommodate everything from

---

457. Matthew 7:21-23
458. Mark 9:38-41; Luke 9:49-50
459. Matthew 12:22-30; Mark 3:22-30; Luke 11:14-23

superstitious evil entities to the malevolent spirits of the departed dead, the hypocrisy of the Pharisees was palpable. Among their favorite litmus tests for the long-expected Messiah was the belief that he would drive out whatever it was they called demons. Yet while not being foolish enough to recognize as Messiah any of the many Jewish exorcists who openly plied their magic trade, the Pharisees nevertheless insisted that Jesus could not possibly be the long-expected Messiah, despite the fact that he obviously drove out demons. Genuine, *talking* demons!

The crowds who witnessed demons being driven out by Jesus were well aware that not a single Jewish "exorcism" could hold a candle to the real thing. When Jesus healed the mute man by driving out the demon within him, the crowd was stunned, saying, "We've never seen anything like this in Israel!"[460]

I have to say that God's providential hand fairly boggles even angel minds. In anticipation of the Son's incarnation and ministry, the Holy One did not shut down Judaism's hodgepodge of beliefs, misguided as their understanding was regarding the true nature of demons. Instead, God turned their superstitious beliefs into a demonstration of Christ's divine authority over both the natural and supernatural world. It's always God's way — taking people where he finds them and giving them a higher vision.

Might this give you some ideas about converting those today who still believe in a world swarming with evil spirits, such as the Hindus and Buddhists of China, Japan, and India, and the animists of Africa and South America? False demonism is as contemporary as it is ancient.

---

460. Matthew 9:32-34

Counterfeit Exorcisms

Making careful distinctions...

and soul Exorcism of a Catholic

What is the difference between exorcisms and driving out demons? In virtually every instance of demon-possession there is a simple, direct command for the evil spirit to depart. No word games, no rituals, no formulas, no set procedures to be followed as would be true of so-called exorcisms. By contrast, driving out evil spirits was a straightforward matter of exerting divine authority over the possessing demons.

However, exerting divine authority did not always come in the form of a direct command to the demon. There was that time, for instance, when Jesus healed the daughter of the Canaanite woman from Syrian Phoenicia without the girl actually being present.[461] Jesus simply told the woman that the demon had left her daughter and she was healed. (We've already mentioned the unusual way in which demons were cast out on one occasion by the apostle Paul.)

I'll save you the next question, which I've heard at least a thousand times! Seems that everyone wants to know why the apostles were unable to drive the evil spirit out of the young boy afflicted with seizures, and why Jesus said "that kind" could be driven out only through prayer.[462] Indeed, Jesus chided the apostles for their lack of faith, which seems odd, given the fact that they had attempted to drive out the demon just as they had been empowered to do.[463] How was this case different from all the others, you ask? And was Jesus really

---

461. Matthew 15:21-28; Mark 7:24-30
462. Matthew 17:14-20; Mark 9:14-29; Luke 9:37-43
463. Matthew 10:1, 8

suggesting that under some circumstances it takes prayer to drive out a demon?

Jesus certainly speaks of prayer, but more so of the need for faith. Strangely, it wasn't that the apostles *lacked* faith, but had *too much* faith...in themselves! Having driven out many demons at that point in their ministry, they had forgotten the source of their power. They had come to assume that all they had to do was say the right words, and out would come the demon. Long gone were those first humbling times when they were keenly conscious of merely being Jesus' emissaries, repeating in his name the simple command that he himself would have given.

Now it was routine. Now it was *their* words, not an act of faith — rather like Moses striking the rock without giving due regard to the source of the miracle.[464] Consequently, this was something the apostles needed to pray about. Or rather, *to be in prayer about* anytime they anticipated driving out demons in the future. To assume they could drive out demons by their own power would be as futile an exercise as the counterfeit ritual exorcisms of their day.

*D*o demons play any role in practices of the occult? Not directly, though demons would happily take credit for it. The occult would not exist were it not for the kind of deception fostered by the Evil One and his cohorts. Why do you suppose Moses' laws forbade divination and sorcery, and the interpreting of omens, and the casting of spells? Why were mediums, spiritists, and those who consult

---

464. Numbers 20:9-12

the dead condemned?[465] What these practices all have in common is an appeal to that which is false. They are all God-substitutes. They are alternative, counterfeit means of seeking knowledge, wisdom, truth, and insight.

It's not that necromancy is just a waste of time since the dead simply do not speak to the living (nor any longer have the slightest clue about life on earth[466]). It's that God alone is to be your source of guidance, not the spirits of the departed dead.[467] Mediums and seances of all sorts may cleverly impersonate the dead, but they can't actually conjure them from Sheol.

The medium of Endor (not really a "witch") was no exception.[468] Her sudden shriek when the spirit of Samuel appeared shows that she was the last one to think she could really and truly make contact with the dead, as she advertised. Only God could have brought up Samuel's spirit to tell Saul the future. It's as true now as it was then: unless God makes it possible, dead men tell no tales!

Nor is it just the prospect of your being fleeced of your hard-earned money by fortune-tellers, soothsayers, and mediums that brings God condemnation. It's that God alone knows the future. Not even demons know the future in the way fortune-tellers, clairvoyants, and mediums claim to know it. To be sure, the Evil One's demonic operatives do know about some things in the future with crystal clarity, like their ultimate destruction. (Remember when the demons nervously asked Jesus if he had come to destroy them *before the set time*?[469]) But

---

465. Deuteronomy 18:9-14; 2 Kings 21:2-6
466. Ecclesiastes 9:5-6, 10
467. Isaiah 8:19
468. 1 Samuel 28:4-25
469. Matthew 8:29; Mark 1:23-24; Luke 4:33-34

fortune-tellers and mediums can't tell you about property prices, or stocks on Wall Street, or which horse is going to win the third race at Santa Anita, else they'd all be millionaires! Why trust them, then, about your future mate, how long you will live, or how to invest your money? More to the point, why consult imposters about anything at all when they couldn't possibly instruct you regarding the really crucial issues of life? Only God knows the future from beginning to end.

So when you read about that poor demon-possessed slave girl being used by her handlers to con people into parting with their money, don't assume she actually had the ability to predict future events.[470] She was a con-artist who was good at what she did because she was possessed by a demon. Which explains why Paul drove the spirit out of her when the girl kept shouting something that was actually quite true — that Paul and his entourage were servants of God telling the people of Philippi the way to be saved. The last thing Paul needed was to have his ministry endorsed by a fortune-teller whom many would have recognized as a con-artist. A known untruthful witness is not to be trusted regarding any specific assertion. Why, then, would Paul welcome support from such a dubious source?

Lest you think that demons are behind every aspect of the occult, I should also tell you that demons were not responsible for Pharaoh's magicians, wise men, and sorcerers being able to replicate some of the miraculous plagues brought by Moses through the power of God. Using their *secret arts* (not demons), Jannes, Jambres, and Pharaoh's other magicians were able to throw down their staffs and have them become snakes. And to turn water into blood, as well as bring frogs out of water onto land.[471] But their magic tricks could not

---

470. Acts 16:16-18
471. Exodus 7:10-12, 19-22; 8:5-6; 2 Timothy 3:8

reproduce gnats, flies, or boils, or the other plagues requiring supernatural power. Even the magicians had to admit it was the finger of God.[472] Had demons been behind their earlier successes, surely the demons' supernatural power could have matched each plague, miracle for miracle.

There were Jewish sorcerers, as well, such as the Cypriot called Bar-Jesus (or Elymas, meaning sorcerer), whom Paul rebuked as being a "child of the devil."[473] But don't assume Paul believed Bar-Jesus to be demon-possessed, or that his sorcery produced real, demonic results. While it would have been easy enough to identify and deal with a demon (as Paul did on other occasions), Paul simply accused Bar-Jesus of being full of deceit and trickery.

You can see it again for yourself when the sorcerers in Ephesus who came to believe in Christ publicly burned their expensive books which detailed mystical occultic formulas and contained all the mumbo-jumbo incantations they had practiced.[474] Nothing to do with demons. It was a secret science. More yet, a bewitching art.

In Samaria, Philip the evangelist encountered a sorcerer who had amazed the crowds with his magic.[475] But Simon the magician instantly recognized Philip's miracles to be in a different league altogether from his clever trickery. Not only did Philip heal paralytics and the crippled, but he also drove out demons. No tricks, no magic. Although Simon got caught up in the excitement and was baptized along with other believers,

---

472. Exodus 8:18-19; 9:10-11
473. Acts 13:6-12
474. Acts 19:17-20
475. Acts 8:4-24

his old habits died hard. Exposing a deeply-flawed character, Simon had the temerity to offer Philip money in order to receive the gift of imparting the Holy Spirit through the laying on of hands. It's obvious that, like many even now, he had been baptized but not converted. It's equally obvious that his magic had no direct connection with demonic activity.

It's fine to "give the devil his due." But giving the devil and his demons *more* than they're due is to distort the truth about them. It is sufficient to accept that the occult is a deceptive hoax from beginning to end. Those caught up in occult practices are not demon-possessed, but deluded. Yet where delusion becomes a fixture in one's life, one risks falling under the sway of the Evil One, becoming as possessed by evil as if demons had literally taken over his body. Play around with the occult, astrology, psychics, and mediums, and you may quickly find yourself in a spiritual abyss of no return.

Want to know what really intrigues me about all of this? It's how the Holy One takes something so normally occultic and turns it into a blessing. Have any idea where I'm going with this one? I'm thinking of the Magi at Christ's birth — those Zoroastrian priests of Persia you call "the Wise Men," who followed that mysterious star to Bethlehem. Linguistically and classically associated with "magic," these Magi were steeped in arcane knowledge, drawn principally from their study of the celestial bodies. Hence, the star. But instead of following a path of superstitious astrology as might have been expected, they followed another light, focusing a never-to-be-forgotten spotlight on the newborn Savior of the world. Love it!

*A*re demons able to perform miracles? Here comes yet another yes-and-no answer. To be able to enter a human body and cause a person harm is certainly a supernatural act which simply has to fall within the category of miracles. So, yes, demons could perform miracles. In his Apocalypse, John even speaks about demons performing miraculous signs.[476] But as you know, demons could not trump the power of Jesus and his emissaries, so their miraculous powers were severely limited in scope. Do not expect demons to bring rain clouds to dampen your parade, or heal the sick (as if they would ever want to!), or raise the souls of your dearly departed.

I see that sparked another question....

Lesson #3

*D*o the spirits of the departed dead ever become demons? *Some of us were taught this* I'm aware that classical writers believed demons to be disembodied spirits of a "pre-Adamite race," but that is faulty on two counts. First and foremost, there was no pre-Adamite race. Read Jesus' lips on that one.[477]

Second, the demons driven out by Jesus and the apostles were not the disembodied spirits of any who have departed this life, either before Adam or since, but rather were fallen angels. The same rebellious angels who lost their place in heaven.[478] The same disobedient angels Peter speaks of as being held in gloomy dungeons.[479] And the same demonic angels John refers to as "locusts" temporarily released from the Abyss.[480]

---

476. Revelation 16:12-14
477. Matthew 19:4
478. Revelation 12:7-9
479. 2 Peter 2:4
480. Revelation 9:1-6

Speaking of Demons

Once the treasonous angels fell, they were known henceforth as demons, in the same way that once a man turns to a life of crime he is called a criminal. Criminal, demon; demon, criminal. There's not much difference. So when your Bible speaks about Satan's angels after the Great Uprising, it invariably refers to them either as "the devil's angels"[481] or as "demons." All other mention of "angels" has reference to righteous, faithful angels.

Don't be misled by the word *spirits*, which Jesus himself used with reference to demons.[482] You will find "spirits" explicitly being used regarding angels, but never regarding the souls of the wicked who have died.[483]

Beware also if anyone should point you to Paul's appearance before the Sanhedrin to argue that demons couldn't possibly be angels because the Pharisees speaking on that occasion referred to both, as if they were two different categories of beings.[484] It's true that the Pharisees were speaking of two distinct kinds of entities—angels on one hand and spirits on the other. But they weren't talking about *evil* spirits, nor certainly *demons*.

Take a second look at that conversation. Hoping to divide and conquer, Paul deliberately asserted his belief in the resurrection, knowing that the Pharisees believed in the resurrection while the Sadducees did not. That did the trick. Suddenly, even some of the Pharisees who previously opposed Paul now saw that they had common cause with him against the Sadducees. Saying they found nothing wrong with what Paul was teaching, they cautioned against opposing him, urging that

---

481. Matthew 25:41; Revelation 12:9
482. Luke 10:19-20
483. Psalm 104:4 (KJV); Zechariah 6:5; Hebrews 1:7 (KJV), 14
484. Acts 23:6-9

what he was saying might have come from an angel or a spirit. As would have been obvious even to the Sadducees, one wouldn't attribute the influence of an *evil* spirit to a position you were affirming as true!

We've already discussed at length that Jewish notions about the spirit world were widely diverse. Since the Pharisees believed in both good and bad spirits, there was no necessary association here between "spirits" and "demons." In this instance, the Pharisees were speaking of benevolent non-angelic spirits. Not that such spirits actually existed. Luke was simply reporting what the Pharisees said without lending credibility to their expansive view of a richly populated spirit world.

If you've read Homer's classics *The Iliad* or *The Odyssey* (both written some six centuries before Christ), you can see how entranced the ancient pagans were with the souls of the dead languishing in a kind of eternal Hades. More than once, Homer's epics take living warriors down into the realm of the dead where "shades" of the dead engage in various conversations with their living visitors. Although the "shades"—both good souls and wicked—seem to be aware of earthly events, never is there any suggestion that they become the kind of malevolent demons Jesus encountered during his ministry. Whatever understanding of demons either the Jews or early Christian converts might have borrowed from the Greeks, nothing suggests they made any connection between the souls of the wicked dead and the demons who were possessing hapless individuals in the first century. More likely, first-century Jews and Gentiles would have thought of the spirits of the departed more like ghosts or apparitions.

It's not unlike what the resurrected Jesus said to his disciples when he suddenly appeared before them in that room with the bolted door. Realizing the disciples thought it must be his ghost, Jesus invited them to touch him, saying, "Ghosts don't have flesh and blood as I have."[485] Did Jesus himself believe in ghosts...as in Casper the Friendly Ghost, or souls of the dead floating around on earth? Not a chance! But he knew *they* did, so he not only invited them to touch his body, but he also ate some fish in their presence to drive the point home even further. (All of this is within your own experience. Come Halloween, and folks who don't believe in ghosts, goblins, or witches will put on costumes as if all those spooky things were real. Or let a man waste away to nothing, and you'll start hearing others speak of him as looking like a ghost.)

This is not to say that people in the first century didn't believe in ghosts. The disciples obviously did, and—as we've already said—so did generations before them, both Jewish and pagan. But Jesus' disciples did not believe in ghosts in any demonic sense. The demons they had contact with were not viewed by them as spirits of the dead—much less the *wicked* dead. If the disciples thought such a thing, you can be sure they would have commanded the "demons" to return immediately to Sheol!

From antiquity, of course, many believed that spirits of the dead, having seen the unseen world, were endowed with superhuman understanding which could be contacted for greater knowledge and wisdom. In time, these "knowing ones" came to be called "demons" and often were even worshiped as gods. You get the connection between false gods and spirits of the dead when the psalmist laments how Israel joined themselves to the Baal of Peor and ate sacrifices to the dead.[486] It was a kind of glorified ancestor worship in which the "gods" were lifeless.

---

485. Luke 24:36-39
486. Psalm 106:28

Angels, Demons, and the Devil

As we've suggested before, the reason necromancy, divination, witchcraft, and seances were all condemned in Moses' Law was not because the dead could actually communicate with the living, but because *the belief that they could* was seductively drawing men's minds away from the one true source of all higher knowledge—which is God.

If you have any lingering doubts about the dead not being able to communicate with the living, remember that it was God, not the medium at Endor, who called up Samuel (a "good spirit") to deliver a prophecy to Saul.[487] And God who called up Moses and Elijah ("good spirits," not "wicked spirits") so that he could speak with the two of them on the Mount of Transfiguration.[488] That's hardly what people are talking about when they suggest that the spirits of the wicked dead have the ability and power to reach from beyond the grave to communicate with the living. But even that is not the most serious issue you need to think about.

What you must not miss is the huge leap from demons being regarded as benevolent departed spirits with superhuman knowledge to demons who are thought to be roaming spirits of the wicked dead malevolently inhabiting the bodies of the living and engaging in spiritual warfare as agents of the Evil One. While the Old Testament verifies the antiquity of the belief in god-like departed spirits, there is not a single report of anyone being possessed by the wicked dead, nor the slightest hint that the spirits of the wicked dead might be up to no good.

Strangely, I don't see anyone advocating that the departed spirits of the *righteous* can inhabit the bodies of the living. If

---

487. 1 Samuel 28:4-19
488. Matthew 17:1-8

the spirits of the dead can leave Sheol for earth, would not one kind of possession be as likely as the other? (Or, are you to believe that only the spirits of the wicked are in Sheol? If that's what you think, think again about the resurrection of the dead—both the righteous and the wicked.[489])

Even though the New Testament assumes a widespread belief in demon-possession in the first century, not a word is mentioned about those demons being the departed spirits of the wicked dead. There's talk of Satan and his angels,[490] but nothing about the wicked dead. Tellingly, Lazarus said not a word upon his sudden return from Sheol about any antics of the wicked dead, nor did the many souls who were raised from the dead at the time of Jesus' own death.[491] If the dead are so aware of what takes place on the other side, as some claim, surely they would have spilled the beans.

It's no secret that for many Jews (and not a few early Christian converts) rumors of demons being the departed spirits of the wicked were rife. So much so, in fact, that Josephus the historian observed that demons were the spirits of wicked men who entered into living men to destroy them, but that they could be driven out by a certain species of root. In the presence of Emperor Vespasian, Josephus personally witnessed an "exorcism" of this type and ascribed its origin as being from King Solomon.

Even at the end of the apostolic age, some of the so-called Church Fathers in the early centuries perpetuated the departed-spirits myth. This should not be surprising. When

---

489. Job 14:12; Matthew 25:31-46; John 3:13; 1 Corinthians 15:12-19, 51-53; 2 Corinthians 5:10
490. Revelation 12:9
491. Matthew 27:50-53

demon-possession became a common phenomenon during the ministries of Jesus and the apostles, it was only natural that many would confuse genuine demon-possession with the ancient idea of demons being departed spirits. But neither Jesus nor the apostles ever gave credence to that foolish notion. You would do well to follow their lead.

*W*hat response would you make to those who deny that demons are fallen angels? Well, I'm certainly aware of the linguistic argument that the ancient pagans never would have made any connection between "demons" and angels since the word *angel* is never found in any ancient pagan literature, only in the Bible. And further that neither Jesus nor his disciples ever explicitly rejected any contemporary understanding of demons by pointing instead to fallen angels. It is true that in Scripture no angel is ever called a demon. Then again, no *faithful* angel *would be* called a demon! Yet it is a bridge too far to expect that Jesus and his disciples went around correcting every false notion of their day. They often used terms with different meanings from those that would be understood by pagan philosophers. Perhaps you'll recall that in Greek mythology Tartarus was a realm of punishment beneath even the Hadean underworld realm of the dead. When that same Greek word (translated as "hell") is used in Peter's second epistle, there is no pretense that Tartarus lies below Uranus, Gaia, and Pontus, as in Plato's *Gorgias*. And Peter doesn't stop to explain the difference.[492]

Naturally, it's always dangerous to make any argument based on what the ancient pagans believed. After all, the pagan philosophers believed in a plurality of gods and demi-gods,

---

492. 2 Peter 2:4-9

many of whom, among other things, had sex with humans, producing human offspring. The pagan gods and demi-gods were also characterized by deception, envy, petty bickering, and power struggles hardly befitting a god of any type. But even without explicitly referring to *angels*, the pagan writers believed in any number of spiritual intermediaries between God and man which were "angels" in all but name.

There's that passage from *The Odyssey*, for example: "...we know the gods go about disguised in all sorts of ways as people from foreign countries, and travel about the world to see who do amiss and who righteously." Or from *The Iliad*: "No man may fight Achilles, for one of the gods is always with him as his guardian angel...." (Naturally, your English translation—"guardian angel"—is post-Christian, but the original conveys the same idea.) And merely consider Plato's *Symposium*, where Diotima tells Socrates that Love "is intermediate between the divine and the mortal...and interprets between gods and men, conveying and taking across to the gods the prayers and sacrifices of men, and to men the commands and replies of the gods; he is the mediator who spans the chasm which divides them." Sound familiar?

The pagans might not have gotten the whole picture right, but since we angels are indeed divine messengers, they were awfully close! And even more so when some of their more corrupt and wicked gods "possessed" various folks–as in *The Iliad* where "The son of Saturn bowed his portentous brows, and Hector fitted the armor to his body, while terrible Mars entered into him and filled his whole body with might and valor." To say the least, it wasn't some wicked person's departed soul that entered Hector!

What you must remember is that the demons with whom Jesus dealt were capable of supernatural powers. Who but us angels — whether righteous or fallen — have such power? Why then should anyone suppose that the spirits of the deceased have a supernatural power in death which they never had in life?

You must also remember that Sheol is not a state of being where you whimsically check in and check out. Not even Satan can "sign you out" for his own dastardly purposes. Until that great Day of Judgment and the resurrection of the dead, nobody who enters Sheol is going anywhere.

*W*as King Saul's "evil spirit" a demon? No, not at all. If you recall, Saul's evil spirit came upon him when the Spirit of the Lord was taken from him — the Spirit which had been given to him as God's first anointed king over Israel. Because of Saul's disobedience, God punished Saul with a troubling spirit of depression, fear, and anger. Occasionally, that tormenting spirit would manifest itself in violent conduct, directed most notably against the young David who eventually would become Saul's successor. Yet, ironically, David's own harp-playing tended to sooth Saul's destructive spirit, as music often does for troubled souls.[493]

If you are looking for cases of "demon-possession," this isn't the best place to look. The only thing this punishing spirit from God had in common with evil, unclean spirits is that they, too, often caused psychological and physical manifestations in their helpless victims. In contrast to the randomly-selected people dominated by demons, Saul had brought on his tormented condition by directly defying God. Indeed, he

---

493. 1 Samuel 16:14-23; 18:10; 19:9

would not be the last person to invite mental anguish into his life for having disobeyed God. Even without direct divine action, the ungodly often reap what they sow — physically, mentally, and emotionally. In such cases, music might *soothe* the soul, but only God's saving grace can *heal* the soul.

If you're wondering whether the "evil spirit" God sent between Abimelech and the citizens of Shechem was anything like Saul's evil spirit, it wasn't.[494] What came between them was neither a demon nor tormenting mental anguish, but merely "bad blood," as you sometimes say. That "bad blood" had been spilt when Abimelech murdered all but one of his brothers.

Nowhere, then everywhere...

*W*hy does the Old Testament have so few references to demons? Great question! As we've discussed already from a number of different perspectives, the writings of the Old Testament reflect a period of virtual inactivity by demons — at least apart from pagan gods and demi-gods called "demons" (worse yet, "devils").

The demons associated in the New Testament with Satan's rebel angels are absent from the Old Testament for the simple reason that they took no part in that period. (Even the Evil One was limited to rare terrestrial forays during that period, such as the time he confronted me over Moses' body. Even then, he was allowed no personal contact with humankind.) So where were his angels during that time, you ask? As we've

---

494. Judges 9:23-25

noted, they were confined in the Abyss, awaiting the time when they would be released for a brief while on a short leash.

A picture not unlike what actually happened is vividly painted in John's Apocalypse. In his vision, as you will know, John sees a star coming out of heaven with a key to the Abyss. When the Abyss is unlocked, from out of the rising smoke come hordes of locusts having the power of scorpions to torment people on earth, although under strict limitations of time and circumstance. You'll not be surprised that their king is the Angel of the Abyss.[495]

What John's fantastic vision depicts is in line with what actually occurred. When Jesus Christ came into the world, rebel angels from the Abyss were permitted to enter into the world as demons capable of tormenting humans with various diseases and mental aberrations. As I indicated previously, this carefully circumscribed demonic visitation was allowed in order for Jesus and his chosen emissaries to demonstrate Christ's divine authority over even supernatural powers.

In their own bumbling, superstitious way, the Jews were actually right about the coming Son of David and his power to vanquish demons. So as to remove all doubt about Jesus' Messiahship, the "war in heaven" was being waged all over again—this time on a different field of battle, this time between the forces of the Evil One and the Son. As with the "war in heaven," so too this battle would not last forever. In the timelessness of eternity, it was but a brief interval. But what a crucial interval it was indeed!

---

495. Revelation 9:1-11

*I*s this why the New Testament has so much to say about demons? It's not just the cosmic conflict with the Evil One that was so important, but—as with all of Jesus' miracles, yet even more so—the driving out of demons was a demonstration of the divine power behind Jesus' ministry. As important as compassion was to Jesus' ministry, his miracles of healing were rarely done for the sole purpose of showing compassion. Otherwise, Jesus would have healed *all* of the sick and dying. Rather, Jesus' miracles were a powerful, dramatic way of confirming him as the Son of God, and assuring that his teaching was divine truth. So there was always a vital connection between miracles and preaching. The object of the exercise, first and foremost, was always *the good news of salvation come down to man.*

Of all Jesus' miracles, his mastery of the supernatural was always more persuasive than his control over the forces of nature, powerful as those miracles were. Turn water into wine? Not a problem. Cause a tempestuous sea to be calm? Easy. Heal the sick and raise the dead? All in a day's work, even for God's prophets. But demonstrating dominance over *supernatural* beings was a power no prophet had ever exercised. This power was radically different. This power was special. To all but the spiritually calloused, this power was convincing!

What to some might be little more than a throwaway line ("Jesus traveled throughout Galilee, preaching in synagogues and driving out demons") could not have been more significant.[496] It's all that need be said, really. Driving out demons was the ultimate authentication of Jesus' gospel. Little wonder the New Testament highlights Jesus' interaction with demons in such great detail.

---

496. Mark 1:38-39

*H*ow did the demons know Jesus was the Holy One of God? That's simple. As angels formerly around the heavenly Throne, the wicked rebels knew the One God (Son as well as Father), "up close and personal," as I believe you say. Which explains why, despite their rebellion (or maybe all the more so *because* of it), the demons not only believe, but shudder.[497] Yet in the fashion of many humans, the demons only "believe" by way of reluctant acknowledgment, and "shudder" out of raw fear rather than awe.

What's important here is how, without being asked, the demons so eagerly announced who Jesus was (even if in Gentile regions they sometimes spoke of him as the Most High God, a distinctly Gentile expression).[498] That Jesus told the evil spirits to be quiet (until his time had come) should not overshadow the fact that these supernatural testimonies came unprompted from the demons themselves. It wasn't for *their* benefit, but for anyone thereafter doubting who Jesus was. As dubious as the testimony from demons normally would be, even liars sometimes tell profound truths — particularly when (as in your law) it's an admission against personal interest.

Oh, and one more thing. As a tag to our earlier conversation, you can be dead certain that demons could never be the wicked spirits of departed *atheists*, since demons believe in God. They believe because, as fallen angels, they have seen God face to face. Not so the souls of the dead in Sheol — whether righteous or wicked.

This matter of possession...

---

497. James 2:19
498. Matthew 8:29; Mark 1:23-25; 5:7; Luke 8:28

*W*hy do the Scriptures never use the term *demon-possession*? Maybe the better question is why so many today refer to *demon-possession* when the Scriptures never use that term. Either way it's not a matter of great concern. We all know what we're talking about when we use the term, and the phenomenon itself is well defined in Scripture.

In fact, it is to assure our being on the same page that the terms *possessed*, *demon-possessed*, and *demon-possession* are most frequently used. To say that a person is "demonized" is certainly correct (and reflective of the original word, *daimonizomai*), but the intended meaning for "demonized" might well run the gamut all the way from a demon literally inhabiting and controlling a person to influencing a person externally in some lesser way. To be possessed by a demon is not necessarily to have every aspect of one's life under a demon's control, but certainly it is to act involuntarily, and possibly to suffer physically or mentally.

"Possession," then, is the unique indwelling of a demon, which is variously described in the Gospels and Acts as a person *having* a demon,[499] or as a demon having gone *into* a person.[500] Which corresponds neatly with the idea of a possessed person being "dispossessed" of the demon by having it *driven out*.[501] Believe me, the demons themselves would know the crucial difference between influence and possession. When possession was involved, it was always a case of forced eviction!

---

499. Matthew 11:18
500. Luke 8:30
501. Matthew 9:33

Angels, Demons, and the Devil

*H*ow could people tell when a demon had been driven out? In most instances, the demons would let out a blood-curdling shriek, or violently shake their victims, or throw their victims down to the ground.[502] Sometimes all of the above! Never fear, the people who witnessed demons being driven out were left in no doubt about what had happened!

*I*s demon-possession related to sin? No way. Victims of demon-possession during the ministry of Christ and his apostles were selected at random by the demons. They were not chosen because of any particular sin or deficiency in character. There was, for example, that father who begged Jesus to deal with the demon causing his son to have epileptic fits. The son was still an innocent toddler when, "from childhood," he was brought under the evil influence of his demon dominator.[503] As with all the others healed of demon-possession, there was not a word of rebuke for this young boy's demonic condition.

And there is this to consider as well. Can you think of any instance in which the victim of evil spirits was commanded to *repent*, as would be the case with sin? (Or to renounce Satan?) Look again, and I think you will find that — as with disease and illness — the word most often associated with overcoming demon-possession is *healed*.[504]

---

502. Mark 1:26; Luke 4:35; Acts 8:7
503. Matthew 17:14-21; Mark 9:14-29; Luke 9:37-43
504. Matthew 15:28

Speaking of Demons

*W*as Hitler demon-possessed? Absolutely not! Nor any other infamous butcher of his ilk. Nor vicious criminals or sociopaths or even the common liar. Attributing to demons all heinous acts of sin is to misunderstand demons altogether. When you think about all the biblical accounts of demon-possession, does it strike you that any of the demons caused their victims to sin? There was the girl with the spirit of divination, of course, but can you think of any other instance whatsoever?[505] (We're speaking of *demons* here, not *Satan*.) No doubt Hitler mimicked the demonic in his spiritual rebellion against God, but he was by no means possessed. Just evil. As were his henchmen and all the others who gave his murderous regime aid and comfort.

*C*an you explain why sometimes more than one demon possessed a person? It was a show of force, really—on both sides. For their part, the demons loved to "gang up" on a person just to show they could do it! If one of us is bad news, they reasoned, just how bad is a whole bunch of us!

On one occasion, Jesus capitalized on that very phenomena in response to the demand of the Pharisees that he show them proof of his Messiahship (as if driving out demons wasn't enough!). Refusing to rise to their supercilious challenge, Jesus instead told them the story of a restless demon who, after having been driven out of a man, found no peace in haunting desolate areas and returned with seven of his fellow demons to "set up house" in the man from whom he had been driven out.[506] It was Jesus' way of telling the Jews how hardened their

---

505. Acts 16:16-18
506. Matthew 12:43-45; Luke 11:24-26

hearts were to having peace with God. No matter how many times the nation had gone through a period of restoration and renewal, their restless pursuit of evil had always come home to haunt them—going from bad to worse. (The demons themselves would have loved that story! They revel in being the bad guys, and the more the merrier.)

For his part, Jesus was able to demonstrate all the more forcefully his power over demons when it wasn't merely a one-to-one confrontation, but one against many. It's the same idea, really, as the David and Goliath battle in which the greater the odds against success the more impressive the triumph. Had he wanted to, Jesus singlehandedly could have sent the entire horde of demons packing!

That was the point of the exercise, for example, when Jesus drove the demons out of the crazed man in the region of the Gerasenes. When Jesus asked for a name, the stupefying response was: "My name is 'Legion,' for we are many." Then *he* (the demon) repeatedly begged Jesus not to send *them* (all of them) away.[507] In this instance, you can clearly see the presence of multiple demons, complete with their own spokesdemon!

Having many demons in one person also highlighted the miracle to come—the sending of those demons from the crazed man into the large herd of pigs. Multiple demons can together possess a single body, or scatter into many different bodies. (In fact, I don't know if you've ever noticed it, but Matthew records that there were two men, not just one, who were initially possessed by these demons.[508] Jesus' work that day was doubly cut out for him.)

---

507. Mark 5:9-10
508. Matthew 8:28-34

Speaking of Demons

Along with other women who had been delivered from the power of evil spirits, you'll recall that Jesus' friend Mary Magdalene had been freed from seven tormenting demons.[509] Little wonder that all of those women gave generously and tirelessly in support of Jesus' ministry, but none more than Mary. She who has been delivered of much, serves much. In this case, perhaps seven times as much!

Something else you might not have noticed is a little gem that speaks volumes about Satan's wicked demons. Remember when Jesus drove out an evil spirit in the synagogue at Capernaum? Speaking on behalf of the possessed man *and* himself, the evil spirit cried out, "What do you want with *us*? Have you come to destroy *us*?" As it happens, on that occasion there weren't multiple evil spirits, with one acting as spokesdemon. Rather, there was just pure selfishness disguised as caring altruism. Ever know folks who are constantly couching what they themselves selfishly want in terms of what would be in the best interests of others? Trust me (I well remember this particular demon!), he couldn't have cared less about the man he was possessing. All he was worrying about was saving his own evil skin! (Still think that humans and demons are worlds apart?)

*W*hy did the Jewish leaders accuse Jesus of being possessed? How else could they explain Jesus' miracles apart from acknowledging him as the Son of God? Left in no doubt that Jesus was operating in the realm of the supernatural, the Jewish leaders had only two real choices: Either Jesus was on the good side or the bad side. Refusing to contemplate the implications if Jesus was on the good side, Jesus' detractors were left with no alternative but to

---

509. Mark 16:9; Luke 8:1-3

think the worst of him. Or at least to *accuse* him of the worst. And that they did often.

Remember when Jesus told the Pharisees they belonged to their father, the devil? He was right, of course, but they shot right back, accusing Jesus of being demon-possessed. (*And* a Samaritan. What could be worse!)[510] Nor did it help Jesus' cause when he said that those who keep his word would never die. Given the faithfulness of Abraham and the prophets (all long since dead) Jesus' statement merely confirmed in their minds just how demon-possessed he was!

Never were the Pharisees more desperate than when accusing Jesus of driving out demons by the power of Beelzebub.[511] As Jesus pointed out, it would make no sense for him to be acting on Satan's behalf to drive out Satan's demons![512] But, once convinced he was not the Messiah (much less God incarnate), what else *could* they have said, really? They were between a rock and a hard place.

Then again, the Pharisees were accustomed to demonizing anyone with whom they disagreed, whether or not they performed miracles. Those who rejected John, the immerser, tarred him with the same brush as Jesus. Because John was a long-haired wild man eating locusts and wild honey in the desert, the Pharisees concluded he must have a demon.[513] Or was it because John called them to repent of their self-righteousness, something self-righteous folks never quite see the need for...?

---

510. John 8:39-59
511. Matthew 9:34
512. Matthew 12:22-29; Mark 3:20-30; Luke 11:14-22
513. Matthew 11:18; Luke 7:33

You may be gratified to know that not every Jew agreed that Jesus was possessed by demons. While many insisted that he was demon-possessed and mad as a hatter, others argued that his miracles could not possibly be the works of someone possessed. "Can a demon open the eyes of the blind?" they asked.[514] Good question!

And just in case you think it was only Jesus' first-century disciples who would be "demonized" along with Jesus, think again. It is for you, as well, that Jesus said, "If the head of the family has been called Beelzebub, don't be surprised if it happens to those in his family."[515] Should you find yourself being "demonized" as a disciple of Christ, wear it as a badge of honor.

Current concerns...

*W*hat did Paul mean when he referred to "doctrines of demons"? Two things, really. On one level, Paul was warning that all heresies have their ultimate origin in the world of the demonic. In that sense, all heresies are "taught" by demons. You mortals have an interesting expression that might help here. When you learn from another's actions (as in a golfer watching a previous putt along the same line), I've sometimes heard you say, "I'm going to school on you." It's the same idea here. What the demons have already done, many also do by following in their footsteps.

But Paul had some specific heresies in mind when instructing his young protégé Timothy — namely the teachings about

---

514. John 10:19-21
515. Matthew 10:24-25

celibacy and abstention from certain foods.[516] These instructions were not only for Timothy's benefit, but also for those who would live in later times when seductive teachings would be enjoined upon the church by a false system claiming to speak for God. This same system would introduce heretical teachings *about* demons—particularly those "demons" regarded as spirits of the departed dead. In this case, it's the *righteous* dead to whom homage is paid and prayers are directed, not to mention also the supposed fiery sanctification of the dead in the (unbiblical) state known as Purgatory.

*D*oes demon-possession still occur today? Given all the reports of demon-possession by people of good-will, and particularly by well-meaning, sincere missionaries, I'm certain that the answer I'm about to give you will not be satisfying. To expect demon-possession today, especially as a common phenomenon in certain (mostly animistic) cultures, is both to exaggerate the power of demons and to risk wrongly attributing to demons what might well be explained even without them—often to the harm of innocent victims.

To begin with, beware when "cluster-bombs" start falling from the sky, aimed at the weak and the gullible. When the question is raised as to whether there is demon-possession today, as in the first century, suddenly you begin to hear a muddling cluster of random observations having nothing to do with demon-possession. Such as Timothy's warning that in later times some will follow deceiving spirits and things taught by demons. (Demon-possession?) Or that in 1914 German and Allied armies saw visible angels protecting the British army. (Demon-possession?) Or that a five-year-old was

---

516. 1 Timothy 4:1-5

known to speak obscene profanities from ancient Hebrew. (Demon-possession?) Or people sacrificing to their dead ancestors. (Demon-possession?) Or a three-year-old whose scars on her upper arm have convinced everyone that her parents had given her in marriage to a demon. (Demon-possession?)

Beware when what seems inexplicable to you is easily explained by others as evidence of demon-possession. (New Agers use the exact same phenomena as irrefutable "proof" of reincarnation.) The fact that many religious groups have "documentation" of demon-possession today only means that they have documented what they *interpret* to be demon-possession. Without questioning anyone's sincerity or motives, it has to be said that, from ancient times, pagan religions have just as sincerely believed in all sorts of spirit phenomena which wouldn't pass biblical muster.

The observable data itself is rarely the problem, only the interpretation. Expect demon-possession, and that's likely what you'll get. The corollary to "Be careful what you pray for" is "Be careful what you expect." And then there's this obvious caution: *Calling* something a demon doesn't *mean* it's a demon. It could be any number of physical maladies, or it could be Multiple Personality Disorder or other mental illness, or psychotic behavior. Or repercussions from emotional, physical, or sexual abuse, particularly at a young age. There's no end of available conditions that could give rise to whatever conclusions one might wish to draw.

Which undoubtedly explains why the Roman Church's rules concerning exorcism caution against not believing too readily that a person is demon-possessed. Yet, to take too seriously the "signs of possession" articulated by the Church could lead one to conclude that the apostles themselves were demon-possessed! Merely consider these supposed indicators of demon-possession: the ability to speak in an unknown tongue; the faculty of predicting future events; and powers beyond one's natural abilities. (Where, incidentally, did these tests come from? Did any of the possessed individuals during Jesus' ministry speak in an unknown tongue?)

If one's *form* of driving out demons is biblically suspect, it's a safe bet that these so-called exorcists also have a dubious *understanding* of demon-possession in the first place. In that regard, the Roman Church's rules concerning exorcism are as laced with ritual, incantations, and formulas as the superstitious Jewish exorcisms of Jesus' day.

In contrast to Jesus' simple command for demons to depart, Catholic exorcisms are to be done in a church or other sacred place; the victim is told to fast, where feasible, and is asked whether he renounces Satan (as if to suggest possession is invited); the priest is to have a crucifix in hand...or somewhere in sight; if relics of the saints are available, they are to be applied to the breast or head of the person possessed; the priest is to inquire regarding the name and number of the demons; holy water is to be sprinkled and the sign of the cross applied to any part of the body in acute pain; and any amulets swallowed by the victim to ward off the demon are to be vomited out. Additionally, prayers are to be addressed to God, Christ, the Virgin Mary, and all the apostles and saints; the Sacrifice of the Mass is to be offered, and all bystanders are to be sprinkled with holy water!

So just how convinced are you that this unbiblical religious ritual and church "documentation" is proof of modern-day demon-possession and exorcism?

What you must keep in mind is that the biblical phenomenon of demon-possession was permitted for a specific and limited purpose during the personal ministry of Jesus and his immediate followers. Having power over the supernatural was one of the most convincing means of demonstrating Christ's own divine authority and the derivative authority delegated to his apostles and emissaries in the early church. Wherever the gospel was preached, the message was confirmed by miracles of healing and the driving out of demons.[517]

Because of the singular circumstances underlying that unique period of time, demon-possession took on a crucial importance never to be repeated. (Undoubtedly, you've already noted that nothing is mentioned of demon-possession in the Epistles, which is your first indication of the waning significance of actual demonic activity.)

Even more important is the temporary nature of the demons' release from the Abyss for the specific purpose they were permitted to serve. Once that limited purpose was fulfilled, there was no further reason for demons to operate freely. As evidence of that limitation, the demons themselves trembled at the thought of being sent back to the Abyss.[518] Anything but that, please! They knew they were short-timers. They knew the day would quickly come when they would be cast back down into their gloomy dungeon to await the day of their promised punishment.

Which is a long way of getting to the question behind your question, I suspect: What about Jesus' final words regarding the signs which would accompany those who believe?[519] "Does that

---

517. Matthew 10:7-8; Mark 6:12-13; Luke 9:1
518. Luke 8:31
519. Mark 16:17

apply to *all* who believe?" you ask. "Can believers today drive out demons?" Let me turn the tables, if I might, and ask *you* a question. Can you speak in formal languages you've never been taught, or handle deadly snakes with no fear of harm? For those who would claim the powers of snake-handling and "tongue-speaking" (not to be confused with speaking foreign languages), can they also drink deadly poison with no adverse effects whatsoever? Know any believers who can do that?

Whatever it was that Jesus had in mind as signs accompanying "those who believe," it was a package deal. Not that every believer would do all of these things, of course, but it would be as likely that a believer could survive tangling with a deadly snake or drinking poison as he could drive out demons. So when you hear reports of believers today driving out demons, do you also hear reports of their surviving deadly poison? In the primitive church, there was not just tongue-speaking (glossolalia), but the untutored speaking of other languages.[520] You'll also recall reading how Paul amazed the islanders of Malta when he suffered no harm from the poison viper that coiled itself on Paul's hand.[521] And, of course, demons didn't stand a chance when one of Jesus' followers drove it out in Jesus' name. But none of that was to last.

Once you understand the special purpose for Jesus and his early disciples dealing with demons, and factor in the temporary nature of the demons' release from the Abyss, you can begin to appreciate why the gift of driving out demons had uniquely limited application. Nevertheless, as you sometimes say, "the song may be over, but the melody lingers on." Even from the Abyss, the historical influence of demonic activity has put its stamp on your world for all time. Dabble in the

520. Acts 2:5-12
521. Acts 28:1-6

world, and you'll find yourself dabbling in the demonic. Allow evil to invade your soul, and—even today—you might just as well be possessed by a demon!

*C*an a person be demonized short of being possessed? Not in the particular way I hear people talking about someone being demonized. Even Christians can fall back into the world, which is a spiritual domain created by the Evil One and his demons. So if that's what you're asking about, then I suppose so. But all the talk I hear about someone being "demonized" assumes some aggressive, positive, and direct action by a demon against a specific individual.

Apparently the idea is that when even a Spirit-filled believer gives in to sin, an opening is created through which the devil and his minions can "sneak inside your spiritual armor." This opening occurs, so it is said, when a person sins by deceit, anger, theft, slothfulness, unwholesome talk, bitterness, rage, brawling, and slander. In other words, virtually every sin is an open-door invitation. But it's when one gets addicted to sin, or deeply embroiled in a particular evil, that demonization is supposed to have happened.

For example, how about that young preacher who gets hooked on pornography? Or the godly mother who finds herself repeatedly screaming abuse at her children? Or the elder or deacon whose extramarital affairs have turned him into a serial sex offender? Isn't the problem (so it is argued) that somewhere along the line they have permitted the devil's forces to penetrate their lives...so as to know just how and when to manipulate them into more and more sin?

Angels, Demons, and the Devil

Wow, that's quite a leap! We just went from someone being taken captive by sin (clearly a biblical concept) to someone having demons *literally manipulating them* (but not quite being *possessed!*). And how does one untangle himself from this demonization? It only happens by the power of God, so it is said. Nothing will free the demonized person from recurring sin until the demon has been defeated by the power of Jesus. And how does *that* happen? First, through renunciation of the sin, and then by prayers on behalf of the demonized person, including a plea that the Lord rebuke the demons.

I have to confess that being "demonized" sounds for all the world like being "possessed." A distinction without a difference, really. But that is the least of my concern. When someone is taken captive by a particular sin, it's the *sin* they need to deal with, not some rogue demon from whom they need to be separated physically or spiritually.

When, in his first letter to Corinth, Paul spoke of those who had been held captive by all sorts of sinful lifestyles, he never once mentioned their being "demonized." Nor was there any talk of renouncing demons, or of intercessory prayers calling for the Lord to rebuke demons. Instead, Paul said that these fornicators, adulterers, homosexuals, thieves, drunkards, and swindlers had been washed and sanctified in the name of the Lord Jesus, and by the Spirit of our God.[522] No devil, no demons, just sinful lives...all washed in the blood.

The idea of being "demonized" just short of being "possessed" is not just a mishmash of double-talk. It is wholly without basis in either your Bible or reality.

---

522. 1 Corinthians 6:9b-11

Speaking of Demons

*A*re demons to be feared? Not if you are in Christ. It is enough to be aware of that which is demonic, and to make sure you do not fall under the influence of anything which might be associated with demons. If you are a baptized disciple of Jesus, you will have received the indwelling of the Holy Spirit as you rose up from your watery grave.[523] Unless you knowingly quench that Spirit,[524] no demon could possibly assail your soul to do it harm. Don't forget Paul's encouraging words when he assured the saints in Rome that "neither death nor life, neither angels nor demons, neither the present nor the future, nor any powers, neither height nor depth, nor anything else in all creation, could possibly separate you from God's love in Christ Jesus."[525]

So may it ever be. And so it *will* be!

*S*hould we be concerned about wicked angels? If in asking that question you're assuming wicked angels are somehow different from demons, then you're off on the wrong foot already. Wicked angels, Satan's angels, the devil's angels, and demons are all one and the same. But since so many people misunderstand the connection, let me quash as many rumors as I can about wicked angels.

First, wicked angels do not interfere with the answers to your prayers, as some contend. Do you think for one moment that the Holy One would allow evil beings to prevent communication between himself and his children! For those who are in Christ, the Holy Spirit even intercedes in the prayers of the faithful when words fail.[526]

---

523. Acts 2:37-38
524. 1 Thessalonians 5:19
525. Romans 8:38-39
526. Romans 8:26-27

Second, wicked angels do not help you to sin. Don't be blaming wicked angels for "using you!" And don't think you can win any favor with the Holy One by claiming you were *seduced* to sin by the Evil One. Are you helpless? Have you no control over your actions?

To dismiss the Evil One as the initiating source of your sin is not to suggest that you yourself are inherently evil. You are only evil when you *do* evil, and even then you are not wholly evil. There's no need for overwhelming guilt or self-loathing, just repentance. The only alternative is to play the blame game, as Eve did, desperately trying to foist her sin off on Satan.[527] It didn't work for her, and it won't work for you.

Nor should you believe the rumor that Satan's angels lead people with similar weaknesses to each other so as to increase the odds of their sinning. (Wouldn't that be a convenient excuse for adultery!) Nor should you be gullible enough to swallow the proposition that sociopaths and vicious criminals are surrounded by evil angels who constantly incite them to deviant behavior. Were that the case, it would be the perfect non-responsibility defense, both in the courts of the land and in heaven above.

What's more, wicked angels do not know your special vulnerabilities and tailor temptations to trap you in them. They're not watching you moment by moment to learn your weaknesses. Satan's angels may be supernatural, but they're not God! And they certainly don't know you personally or intimately as does the Holy Spirit. It's true that Jesus knew the thoughts of those around him,[528] but no one else (not even us

---

527. Genesis 3:13
528. Matthew 9:4; Luke 9:47

angels, much less *wicked* angels) knows the thoughts of a person except that person's own spirit.[529]

What's more, don't let anyone fool you into thinking that demon angels (worse yet, wicked spirits of the departed dead) use evil people to harm you, or good people to discourage you, or make you sick, or destroy your property or possessions through tornadoes, hurricanes, or floods. Nor yet (God forbid!) kill you or those you love. Those who would point you to the story of Job as a basis for this belief have misunderstood the nature of the book of Job. And it was a *faithful* angel, not a *wicked* one, whom God (not Satan) dispatched to take Herod's life![530] Whenever wild speculation goes on a spending spree, the first purchase is a pair of glasses that conveniently obscure the crystal clear and the obvious.

About spiritual warfare...

*C*an believers today bind Satan or the demons? In a word, no. They've already been bound! Search your Scriptures high and low, and you'll never find any warrant for believers binding the forces of evil. So-called "deliverance ministries" are skating on thin theological ice indeed to suggest otherwise. Jesus was referring only to himself when he talked about binding the strong man.[531] And Jesus was speaking only to Peter and the apostles when he told them that whatever they bound on earth will already have been bound in heaven.[532] Don't forget that Jesus also said that whatever they *loosed* on earth will have been *loosed* in heaven. Is it

---

529. 1 Corinthians 2:11
530. Acts 12:21-23
531. Matthew 12:25-30
532. Matthew 16:19; 18:18

to be believed that Christians today have either the power or responsibility to set Satan or the demons *loose*? On this occasion, Jesus was not talking at all about the forces of the Evil One, but about kingdom doctrine.

*D*o you have any thoughts about books on spiritual warfare? Let me say, first of all, that I'm thankful for those who recognize and appreciate the ongoing conflict being played out moment by moment in the spiritual dimension. Too many believers are so carnally-minded that it's almost impossible to explain even the most basic truths about a spiritual realm inhabited by angels, demons, and the devil.

But since you asked, I do have some concerns. The most striking impression I have of books on spiritual warfare is that these works start off well, alerting readers to Satan's diabolical strategy, but quickly devolve into a fairly predictable list of sins and evils, all of which could profitably be discussed wholly apart from any direct linkage with the Evil One or his wicked angels.

How does Satan operate, the writers ask? Surely, they respond, Satan takes captives through misleading philosophies and false teachers, and he is the mastermind behind false religions, sects, and cults. And immorality *must be* the work of the Great Deceiver—all of which is true, at least if you get the dynamics right.

Perhaps you have heard this standard spiritual-warfare question: Does not Satan have power over death?[533] Yet the complexity of that seemingly-simple question is rarely explored. Is it *physical* death, or *spiritual* death we're talking about?[534] Does

---

533. Hebrews 2:14-15
534. Romans 5:12, 17

Satan have power over *your* death, by way of either time or circumstance?[535] And didn't Jesus cancel Satan's power through his death on the cross and subsequent resurrection?[536] But, if so, why do humans still die physically? (Consider what Paul was signaling when he said that the last enemy yet to be destroyed is death.[537]) You have much more to think about than is generally assumed in all the books.

Then there are those standard "battle plans" inevitably presented to defeat the spiritual forces of evil. Drawing from familiar passages of exhortation, the writers press the need for more knowledge of the Scriptures, more faith, and more prayer to combat the devil and his demons. And who could deny the value of all those things?

What's lacking, however, is any serious attention to detail—what I might call "the mechanics" of how the Evil One and his angels operate in any direct sense. Despite fervent affirmations that humankind in general, and believers in particular, are engaged in daily combat with the devil, the dynamics of how that happens is rarely spelled out. Most authors repeat a long laundry list of sins which beset man, then quickly conclude that Satan is behind each sin.

As you know by now, I couldn't agree more that there is an important sense in which the Evil One is personally responsible for introducing every sin and temptation known to man. His opening assault in the Garden has had devastating reverberations ever since. But to affirm a direct relationship between distinct, individual sins and some active role being played by the

---

535. Ecclesiastes 9:11-12
536. Colossians 2:13-15
537. 1 Corinthians 15:20-28

Evil One and his entourage is another matter altogether. Were that connection as real as it's typically made out to be, there should be far more explanation of *exactly* how Satan works. Otherwise, how is a believer to fend off the enemy?

For example, are you to believe that Satan arranges for just the right man or woman to come along, causing you to leave your spouse? Or simply penetrates your mind, filling it with lustful thoughts, or anger, or envy, or greed, or pride? Are demonic forces personally sizing you up so as to take advantage of your weak spots? If so, where did they get that power? The fact is, they do none of those things, nor could they!

One would hope for greater thought as to why the Scriptures so often cite individual sins with no hint whatsoever that Satan is actively working behind the scenes to bring about that sin. For example, why does Paul not make even passing reference to the Evil One when commenting on the sin of Jannes and Jambres in opposing Moses?[538] Why is there not the slightest suggestion that the Evil One was behind Korah's rebellion,[539] or Achan's sin at Ai?[540]

We've discussed already the metaphorical sense in which David was "enticed" by Satan to order the offensive census;[541] and also what was meant by Satan "filling Ananias' heart."[542] But what about virtually every other sin recorded in Scripture? Did Satan in some way specifically entice David to lust after Bathsheba?[543] Or literally seduce Solomon into idolatry

---

538. 2 Timothy 3:8
539. Numbers 16:1-35
540. Joshua 7:1-26
541. 2 Samuel 24:1-10; 1 Chronicles 21:1-7
542. Acts 5:3
543. 2 Samuel 11:1-4

through all his pagan wives?[544] Or put into Abraham's mouth the lie he twice told about Sarah?[545] Or somehow convince Peter to deny Jesus?[546] Or cause Paul to kill Jesus' disciples before becoming one himself?[547]

Have you ever asked yourself why in Scripture the Evil One is not always lurking in the shadows—and being specifically identified as the culprit? The reason, as I've repeatedly suggested, is that Satan is not, in fact, *personally* behind every temptation or sin. Nor are his rebel angels. For all the damage the Evil One has done, and for all the ways that the system of evil he introduced in the Garden continues to destroy humankind, Satan himself is not your worst enemy. Moment by moment, temptation by temptation, sin by sin, *you* are your own worst enemy!

So there's not really a spiritual war going on? No, no. There is indeed a war going on, and you live on the front line. Spiritual warfare is the right idea. Spiritual artillery is flying in your direction this very moment in the form of temptations from the world to submit to its God-denying values. If you wish to attribute those assaults to the Evil One as the one who drew up the original battle plan, then you'd be right. But you needn't worry that he's sitting right beside you as we talk.

The grand irony is that most spiritual warfare books so distort the true nature of spiritual warfare that believers are left all

544. 1 Kings 11:1-8
545. Genesis 12:10-20; 20:1-18
546. Matthew 26:69-75; Mark 14:66-72; Luke 22:55-62; John 18:15-18; 25-26
547. Acts 8:1a; 26:9-11

the more vulnerable to Satan's schemes. To suggest that the Evil One and his gang of angels can actually produce *more than they really can* is to undermine what they *actually can do*. To turn the devil into a character so comedic that he becomes a laughing stock is to permit his being dismissed altogether. To paint too terrifying a picture of him is to make believers more fearful and less confident than they need be. To find him behind every rock and rock concert is to give him way too much time on stage.

Don't give the Evil One the pleasure of being thought omnipresent, or omniscient, or omnipotent — all of which attributes are virtually assumed by most spiritual warfare literature. Satan only *wants to be* God!

It's *balance* that's needed when you put on the full armor of God to combat the forces of evil in your world.[548] The extreme that denies (if only in practice) the existence of any spiritual battle whatsoever is out of touch with reality. (If only they knew what *I* know!) Yet the opposite extreme — the one that puts Satan on a virtual par with the divine power of the Sovereign God — ironically accomplishes for the Evil One what he most desires but has never been able to accomplish for himself!

For you and other believers, spiritual warfare is not being waged primarily against invisible evil beings, but by the invisible spiritual forces championed by those invisible evil beings. For you, the war of Satan's aggression is fought in the familiar trenches of the shopping mall where consumerism threatens to consume its consumers. In the inner city where fathers are abandoning their children, leaving them vulnerable to drugs, violence, and ignorance. In middle-class (Christian!) families,

---

548. Ephesians 6:13

where divorce is wreaking untold havoc. In the schools, where God's holy name has been banished. In the sterile clinics of mass destruction around the world where the greatest-ever crime against humanity snuffs out a precious life every five seconds. In the media, where the minds and morals of even the most dedicated believers are unceasingly polluted. In higher education, where the supernatural is scoffed at, and academic hubris is only slightly less prideful than the Evil One himself. And even in churches, where empty religious ritual robs the cross of its power. Need I go on?

The spiritual warfare you must fight is not normal warfare. Your weapons are not the world's weapons, which can blow up cities and destroy armies. By God's grace, you have the power to disarm every force of evil seeking to take you captive and, instead, be obedient to Christ.[549]

What you need most is not some cleverly contrived, artificial strategy to defeat a force that (but for the grace of God) you couldn't stand up to if he set his mind to destroy you. What you need most is simply to keep yourself pure and faithful. Stay in the Word, yes; and call in prayer support to counter each incoming attack. But don't forget that the Evil One himself is *bound*!

As are the demons. For when the Son was resurrected, he ascended into heaven where, even now, he sits at the Holy One's right hand (as it were), with all things under submission to him. That includes not only us faithful angels happily in submission, but also all the rebellious authorities and powers in reluctant submission to him from within the Abyss.[550] In every

---

549. 2 Corinthians 10:3-5
550. Psalm 110:1; Matthew 28:18; Ephesians 1:18-23;
    Colossians 2:9-10, 15; Hebrews 2:5-9; 1 Peter 3:21b-22

possible permutation of submission, Christ the Son *has already bound, is even now binding*, and *will forever bind* the Evil One and his demon angels.

Naturally (as the Hebrew writer notes[551]), you are not presently able to *see* that unseeable submission. For until Christ comes again, the system of sin that the Evil One introduced to this world will remain in full, shocking view. But never fear. For Satan and the demons, the fat lady has sung (to use your colorful expression), and the ball game is over! All that remains is for human death to be swallowed up in victory at the Resurrection, and for the Evil One and his demons to be destroyed eternally in the "fiery lake." At that point, the Son will hand over his authority to the Father, making the One God all in all.[552]

Meanwhile, in the Abyss of Tartarus, the utter defeat of Satan and his angels is a matter of utmost chagrin and no little second thought, I can tell you. Do you recall in the story of Esther how the wicked Haman ended up being hanged on gallows he himself had ordered built?[553] Self-destruction is always the undoing of the wicked, and never more so than on a day of unparalleled significance at Golgotha. On a cross cruelly envisioned by the Evil One himself, Christ turned the tables, and forever defeated Satan and his angels. Even now, the Lord reigns in a holy heaven cleansed of all sin and rebellion. And all together we angels cry, "Holy! Holy! Holy!" May the same forever be true of your own heart: cleansed and holy. *Wholly* holy.

The next time we meet—and it won't be long now—there'll be no more talk of demons and the devil. By then, their fate will

---

551. Hebrews 2:8
552. 1 Corinthians 15:24-28
553. Esther 7:9-10

have been forever sealed. Regarding us angels, there'll be no need of more questions. All will be known. Every mystery revealed. Every misconception corrected.

Just promise me you won't be too disappointed about our having no wings. On the other side, I'll show you some celestial moves that will absolutely astound you! That is, if you can ever take your adoring eyes off the Holy One....

Angels, Demons, and the Devil

Scripture References

Scripture References

Angels, Demons, and the Devil